"*Guided By Grace* is a testimony of faith, resilience, and courageous leadership in the face of organizational inertia. With the voice of a storyteller, the heart of a pastor, and the mind of a scholar, Keith Haney weaves together parable and strategy, bringing to life the principles of organizational change in the local church. Whether you are a church leader or congregational member, this book will unpack and help you navigate familiar tensions such as wandering in the wilderness of tradition and change."

—Eugene P. Kim, Professor of Leadership and Organizational Change, Concordia University Irvine

"Dr. Haney has written the definitive 'how to' leadership manual that will guide congregations to discover how they can preserve their unique traditions while prayerfully discerning how to serve well those whom God has placed in their path. Through the telling of the story of Calvary Church, Haney adroitly allows the reader to unpack and understand his or her own congregation. *Guided By Grace* is a perfect resource for pastors and their congregational leaders to read together."

—Kurt Senske, author of *The CEO and the Board: The Art of Nonprofit Governance as a Competitive Advantage*

"I appreciate Rev. Dr. Keith Haney's creative approach in providing a proven process for leading congregational change. The heart of *Guided by Grace* is a fictional narrative. However, the story is drawn from Haney's real-life experiences in more than thirty years working with congregations and church leaders. By closing chapters with practical guidance and exploratory questions Haney makes *Guided by Grace* a practical handbook for church leaders facing today's challenges."

—Kevin Wilson, President, Ohio District Lutheran Church Missouri Synod

"*Guided by Grace* is both thoughtful and deeply relatable. Through a compelling narrative, Haney captures the real challenges that church leaders face when trying to lead meaningful change. What makes this book stand out is its honest portrayal of the emotional, spiritual, and practical realities of ministry. It does not offer quick fixes. It offers wisdom, reflection, and real tools rooted in lived experience. I felt a deep sense of connection while reading and was encouraged by the steady reminder of why this work matters. This is a valuable resource for anyone committed to helping their congregation grow while staying grounded in faith."

—Kellie Albrecht, Assistant Dean, Concordia University Irvine

Guided By Grace

Guided By Grace

A Narrative to Lead Organizational Change

BYRENE K. HANEY

RESOURCE *Publications* • Eugene, Oregon

GUIDED BY GRACE
A Narrative to Lead Organizational Change

Copyright © 2025 Byrene K. Haney. All rights reserved. Except for brief quotations in critical publications or reviews, no part of this book may be reproduced in any manner without prior written permission from the publisher. Write: Permissions, Wipf and Stock Publishers, 199 W. 8th Ave., Suite 3, Eugene, OR 97401.

Resource Publications
An Imprint of Wipf and Stock Publishers
199 W. 8th Ave., Suite 3
Eugene, OR 97401

www.wipfandstock.com

PAPERBACK ISBN: 979-8-3852-5166-7
HARDCOVER ISBN: 979-8-3852-5167-4
EBOOK ISBN: 979-8-3852-5168-1

Thanks to my family (Mitchell, Todd, Sharon, Jonathan, SaraGrace, Zane, Zipporah, Vincente, Mateo and Nalah) for all the support you have shown me throughout this book. It represents the culmination of three years of doctoral learning, transforming that knowledge into a resource for the church. This is a special tribute to my wife, Miriam. You are my rock. Thank you for your unwavering support. Your faith in me has never faltered. Without my greatest cheerleader, I would have stopped dreaming long ago. You have been amazing, and I will now clear all the papers in the living room until I start my fourth book.

Contents

Acknolwedgments ix

Author's Note xi

Introduction xiii

Chapter 1: A New Beginning: Arrival in Oakridge 1

Chapter 2: Crossroads of Faith: Navigating Tradition and Change 16

Chapter 3: A Voice of Wisdom: The Search for a Mentor 27

Chapter 4: Building Bridges: Forming the Core Team 40

Chapter 5: Forging the Path Forward 55

Chapter 6: Facing the Storm 69

Chapter 7: Tears and Fears 80

Chapter 8: From Conflict to Community 98

Chapter 9: Guided Through the Wilderness 114

Chapter 10: A Community Reborn 126

Acknowledgments

I want to thank the following people, without whom I would not have completed this doctoral research, earned my doctor's degree, and then turned that information into this resource for churches!

The dissertation Committee at Concordia University, Irvine, especially my Chair, Dr. Eugene Kim, whose insight and knowledge into the subject matter steered me through this research. I also thank Dr. Dwight Doering, who talked me into starting this doctoral process. He saw something in me that I did not see in myself. And special thanks to Rev. Dr. Kevin Wilson, whose prayers, encouragement, and support allowed my studies to go the extra mile.

My colleagues, the Board of Directors at Iowa District West, and the churches that allowed it to be a training ground for growth. Thank you, Berea Lutheran Church, Detroit, MI, St. Matthew and St. Stephen's in Walnut Park and St. Louis, and especially Gospel Lutheran Church in Milwaukee we had a great run. You have supported me and endured my pushing the limits and growing pains as we tried to figure out how to do ministry in an urban context.

Author's Note

In crafting this book, my goal was to provide a comprehensive and practical guide to organizational change within a church setting. Each chapter is meticulously structured to ensure that readers not only understand the theoretical aspects of change but also see how these concepts are applied in real-life scenarios.

Chapter Structure:

1. **Introduction to the Organizational Change Process:** Each chapter begins with a detailed paragraph that introduces the specific organizational change process being discussed. This section sets the stage by explaining the importance and relevance of the change process within the context of church operations.

2. **Narrative Account of Calvary Church:** Following the introduction, the chapter transitions into a narrative account of how the change process was implemented at Calvary Church. This story-based approach allows readers to visualize the practical application of the concepts. By sharing the experiences, challenges, and successes of Calvary Church, readers gain a deeper understanding of the dynamics involved in organizational change.

3. **Recommendations and Insights:** Embedded within the narrative are recommendations and insights that further elucidate the change process. These suggestions are designed to provide actionable advice and highlight best practices that can be adapted to other church settings.

4. **Conclusion with Recommendations and Questions:** Each chapter concludes with a set of recommendations and thought-provoking

questions. These elements are intended to encourage reflection and discussion, helping readers to critically assess their own situations and consider how they might apply the lessons learned to their own church environments.

Purpose and Vision:

The structure of the chapters is intentional and serves several key purposes:

- **Clarity and Understanding:** By starting with a clear explanation of the change process, readers are equipped with the foundational knowledge needed to grasp the subsequent narrative.
- **Practical Application:** The narrative account provides a real-world example, making the theoretical concepts more relatable and easier to understand.
- **Actionable Advice:** Recommendations within the narrative and at the end of each chapter offer practical steps that readers can take to implement similar changes in their own churches.
- **Engagement and Reflection:** The concluding questions are designed to foster engagement and encourage readers to think critically about their own organizational practices.

Through this structured approach, I aim to provide a valuable resource that not only educates but also inspires and empowers church leaders to navigate and implement effective organizational change.

Thank you for embarking on this journey with me. I hope that the insights and stories shared in this book will be both enlightening and transformative for your church community.

Introduction

Churches push and pull against cultural and social trends; this resistance negatively affects churches and people because they struggle to remain relevant in a rapidly changing society. As society moves further away from church culture and the church becomes less critical in people's daily lives, the organization needs to change its approach to the disenfranchised. However, the foundation of the Gospel, God's plan for salvation, remains vital to its core. The Gospel message is still unchanging and powerful, but the organizational structure and strategies are slow to adapt to the demands of change.

Churches often grapple with balancing tradition and modernity, as long-standing customs and practices clash with contemporary societal expectations. Congregations usually resist altering established norms, leading to internal conflict and division. Moreover, leadership may struggle with finding ways to effectively communicate the timeless message of the Gospel in a manner that resonates with younger, more diverse audiences.

Churches struggle because they do not adapt to change quickly. This realization comes from the author's own first-hand experience. My organizational change journey began when I graduated from the Seminary in 1993, was ordained, and was called to a congregation at Berea Lutheran Church in Detroit, Michigan. It was a congregation, like many, that was stagnating and declining. Sixty percent of Protestant churches have plateaued or declined in attendance, and more than half saw fewer than ten people become new Christians in the past 12 months. These numbers match the trends many of the class of '93 would face. I know these statistics scream danger as someone involved in congregational change for over thirty years.

My experience highlights the challenges of organizational change in churches. Many congregations are stagnating or declining, with over half

Introduction

seeing fewer than ten new converts joining their ranks annually. Despite the urgency, many churches deny or minimize the need for change, often skipping critical steps in the process. This approach leads to resistance and poorly planned initiatives, furthering the decline.

Creating a situation where the church needs to experience a season of Holy Discontent is essential for successful change. This Holy Discontent is a visible crisis that can motivate people to act. I learned from early mistakes that change efforts falter without buy-in from leaders and congregation members. Resistance to change, deeply rooted in fear, uncertainty, or complacency, poses significant risks.

After fifteen years on the frontlines of ministry, I have spent the second half of my ministry career working at the middle judicatory level. I have helped congregation members and leaders find an effective organizational change process. That journey landed me on district teams in Northern Illinois and Western Iowa. Even though I tried my best, I could not change the church's attitude. While it was not labeled Holy Discontent at the heart of the process, that was the end goal.

Unfortunately, the results were inconsistent. Some congregations shifted from languishing to flourishing, and others started out strong, but the day-to-day challenges of ministry sucked the passion and energy out of the change process. With some time, distance, and armed with new tools, I see the errors or limitations of jumping to vision too soon or introducing a ministry plan without getting key leadership on board. A wise man once said, "If you are leading and no one is following you, then you are simply taking a walk." And a long walk of a short plank is unsuitable for long-term ministry viability.

With 75 percent of the congregations I worked with were either plateauing or declining, the need for change becomes more urgent. During my thirty-plus years of serving the church at this level and making connections with over 300 congregations, the need to lead them to a flourishing model of ministry is clear. Still, the resistance to change is also daunting.

Without enthusiasm for the future, people tend to be very nostalgic for the past. Nostalgia can heavily influence decision-making by causing individuals to idealize past experiences and resist change. This often leads to a preference for familiar solutions rather than innovative approaches. As a result, people may miss opportunities for growth and adaptation in favor of maintaining the status quo.

INTRODUCTION

Embracing change, however, opens the door to new opportunities and allows individuals to develop resilience and adaptability. People can discover more efficient solutions and enhance their personal and professional growth by welcoming innovation. This forward-thinking mindset fosters creativity and prepares individuals and organizations to flourish in an ever-evolving world while maintaining the Gospel truth and power.

1

A New Beginning: Arrival in Oakridge

Every minute, hour, and day of your life represents a new beginning. The journey starts now—not tomorrow, next week, or next year.

Holy Discontent

> When a church begins any major organizational change it begins with an acknowledgement of the realities ahead. This could best be described as a season of holy discontent. When we experience holy discontent, we are aligned with God's heart for taking positive action to change the world. We have an uneasy spirit about the brokenness of this world. It may result in the loss or change in institutional identity. The loss of change leads people to react as they would when grieving. This sense of loss can lead to the failure of the change process and the eventual closure of the institution. In order to measure the impact of this loss among key stakeholders. The leader is encouraged to communicate potential mission opportunities due to this change clearly.

The winding country road stretches out before Pastor Terrance McAllister, unfurling like a ribbon of possibility. With each curve, he catches another beautiful glimpse of the rolling hills surrounding Oakridge. His hands grip the steering wheel, knuckles a bit white with a mix of excitement and nervous energy.

"Look, Beth," he says, nodding towards a particularly picturesque vista. "It's like Psalm 121 comes to life. 'I lift up my eyes to the hills—where does my help come from? My help comes from the Lord.'"

Beth smiles, her chestnut hair glowing in the afternoon light. "It's beautiful, Terrance. A perfect place for new beginnings."

As Terrance glances in the rearview mirror, he sees his son, Grant, quietly dreaming in his car seat. The sight of the little one brings a deep sense of purpose to his heart. This journey isn't just about fulfilling his calling; it's about building a legacy of faith for his family.

As they round the final bend, Calvary Church comes into view, and Terrance feels a wave of emotion. The building stands proudly against the scenic hills, its white clapboard siding telling stories of years spent in sun and rain. The steeple leans a bit, like it's gently bowing to the passing of time.

Terrance parks his car in the gravel lot, the crunch of stones beneath the tires mirroring the flutter of emotions in his heart. As he steps out, feeling somewhat stiff from the long drive, he takes a deep breath and embraces the view of his new endeavor with a mix of excitement and curious anticipation.

"Well, what do you think?" Beth asks, coming to stand beside him.

Terrance runs a hand through his dark hair. Up close, his eyes can more readily see the peeling paint and sagging gutters. "It's... it's got character," he says, trying to infuse his voice with more confidence than he feels.

Beth squeezes his hand. "It's a diamond in the rough, just waiting for someone to bring out its shine." Her encouraging words lift him up, Terrance nods at her and smiles. As Terrance nears the church steps, a hint of doubt begins to sneak in. The old wooden boards groan beneath his feet, a reminder of the hurdles that may be waiting for him. He takes a moment at the door, his hand hovering over the faded brass handle. "Lord," he whispers, closing his eyes briefly, "Guide my steps. Let this be the beginning of something extraordinary."

With a deep breath, Terrance pushes open the door, the hinges groaning in protest. The musty scent of old hymnals washes over him. Sunlight filters through stained glass windows, casting kaleidoscope patterns on worn pews. "It's like stepping back in time," Beth murmurs, cradling a now-awake Grant against her hip. Terrance nods, his mind already racing with ideas. "Maybe that's part of the problem," he muses. The building is in much worse physical shape than I was anticipating. It reminds me of our home

A New Beginning: Arrival in Oakridge

church, the physical decay was a visible reminder of a deep fiscal issue. To move this church forward it will take patience and care as "We honor the past while moving boldly into the future."

Terrance feels a sense of responsibility hanging over his shoulders as he stands in the quiet sanctuary. He seems to sense the possibilities and challenges ahead in the stillness around him. In his reflection, he remembers Pastor Victor Klaus, whose brief and eventful tenure here still resonates through these walls, and Pastor Roger Craig, whose long service witnessed the gradual changes in this once-thriving church. "We have our work cut out for us," Terrance says, his voice carrying a mixture of determination and uncertainty. Terrance is concerned about the building's condition. His home church had similar warning signs. Due to financial restraints, the trustees faced a major roof repair right before the church closed. This roof repair was the tipping point that led to the church's closure.

Beth moves a little closer, wrapping her free arm around his waist. "We're in this together, with God's loving guidance and strength." Terrance nods, feeling uplifted by her comforting presence. Grant begins to giggle and reaches out to his daddy. In this heartfelt moment, surrounded by the gentle beauty of Calvary Church, he senses a spark of hope—a small flame, waiting to grow into a vibrant fire of renewal and faith.

The creak of the old floorboards signals Pastor Roger Craig's arrival. Terrance looks up to meet the kind gaze of a man whose weathered face tells the story of a life dedicated to service. Despite the signs of weariness in his eyes, there's a brightness of warmth. Roger reaches out his hand in a welcoming gesture. "Welcome to Calvary, Pastor McAllister," Roger says, his voice carrying the gentle timbre of a well-worn sermon. "I trust you found your way without too much trouble?"

Terrance gives Roger's hand a warm, firm shake, his youthful energy contrasting with the older man's wise demeanor. "Thank you so much, Pastor Craig! The drive was absolutely beautiful, though I have to say, the church is a bit different from what I was expecting. In the communications with the search committee, they made it sound like this was a healthy church, that was passionate about reaching young families, wanting to connect with members who had strayed and looking to move forward. They talked about the history and how important the legacy of this building was to them and the community. So, to find it and the mission drift was shocking."

Terrance's words hung in the air, a mix of curiosity and concern evident in his tone. Pastor Craig's eyes softened as he nodded, understanding the young man's surprise. "I can see how you might feel that way, Terrance," he began, his voice calm and reassuring. "This church has indeed faced its challenges, and the mission drift you mentioned is something we've been grappling with. But that's precisely why we need fresh perspectives and new energy like yours. Together, we can work towards revitalizing our community and realigning with our core values. It's a journey, but one worth taking."

Roger gives a gentle smile that wavers a bit. "Ah, yes! Time has taken its toll on our cozy sanctuary and we have lost our connection to the community. Calvary has been a church guided by a strong traditional approach to ministry. Calvary's traditional worship style is characterized by a deep-rooted sense of reverence and simplicity. The services often feature hymns and handbells, creating a serene and reflective atmosphere. The choir, though small and struggling, adds a heartfelt touch to the worship experience. Children are expected to sit through the sermon, fostering a sense of discipline and involvement from a young age.

All church events are held on the church's campus, emphasizing community and continuity. Calvary prides itself on being a "meat and potatoes" Bible-teaching congregation, focusing on straightforward, unembellished teachings of the Bible. They maintain a purist stance, deliberately avoiding influence from outside cultural trends to preserve their traditional values and practices. Calvary needs to examine its mission and chart a new path forward and that is exactly why you've been called to serve, right? You have a heart and passion for those disconnected from God. You are here for a time such as this."

As Beth excuses herself to tend to Grant, Terrance and Roger settle into a nearby pew. The older pastor's demeanor shifts, his shoulders sagging under an invisible weight. "I will be candid with you, brother," Roger commences, his tone subdued and infused with a sense of remorse. "We find ourselves in a precarious situation. Over the past several years, attendance has consistently declined. This past Sunday, scarcely sixty individuals were present in the worship service."

Terrance's heart sank as he absorbed Roger's words. The reality of the church's struggles hit him hard, and he felt a mix of frustration and determination. He had envisioned a vibrant community, but the stark truth was far from his expectations. "I understand, Pastor Roger," Terrance replied, his voice steady but tinged with concern. "It's disheartening to see such a decline. We need to find ways to reconnect with the congregation and bring new life into our services. It's going to be a tough journey, but I'm committed to working through these challenges with you."

As Terrance looks at the elders' records for attendance he notices that the numbers they recorded has shown a steep decline. It appears that no one has updated the church body with the correct numbers for several years. There was a mass exodus of members three years ago. Several members transferred their membership or just left the church altogether. About that same time the financial situation also tanked. Terrance nods, his brow furrowing. "I understood there were challenges, but I had no idea it was this severe. It is not merely a matter of occupancy; our financial situation is dire. We are struggling to cover basic operational costs, much less the maintenance of the facility or the continuation of outreach programs."

Listening to Roger, Terrance's mind becomes increasingly agitated. He reflects on the dynamic ministry he had envisioned and the community outreach initiatives he had meticulously planned. How can he instigate change when the very foundation is in a state of disarray?

Terrance took a deep breath, trying to steady his thoughts. "Pastor Roger," he began, his voice firm but respectful, "I believe we can turn this around. It won't be easy, but we need to start by understanding the root causes of this decline. Perhaps we can hold a series of listening sessions with the congregation to hear their concerns and ideas. We need to show them that their voices matter and that we're committed to revitalizing this church together. But first, we need to get the church to a point of acknowledging the current state of the church. Only then can we begin to make meaningful changes."

Roger nodded slowly, a glimmer of hope in his eyes. "You're right, Terrance. It's time to take bold steps and re-engage with our community. Let's start planning those sessions and see where we can make the most impact."

Terrance felt a renewed sense of purpose. Despite the challenges ahead, he was determined to breathe new life into Calvary and build a stronger, more connected congregation

In a subdued tone, Roger continues. "The most challenging aspect is the resistance from the congregation. Numerous remaining members are accustomed to their established ways. The prospect of change induces apprehension within them, particularly following the incident involving Pastor Klaus." He paused, his words guarded. He did not want to defame a brother pastor. Roger reflected on the weight of past events and trauma. "Pastor Klaus tried to introduce some modern elements to our services, but it didn't go well. Many felt it was too abrupt and against our traditions. The backlash was intense, and it ultimately led to his departure. Since then, there's been a lingering fear of change, making it even harder to move forward."

Terrance leans in, curiosity piqued. "Pastor Klaus? I'm not familiar with that name."

Roger inclines his head in a subtle gesture of dissent, revealing a trace of melancholy in his gaze. "This narrative may be better suited for a future occasion.." Terrance processes this information, grappling with the conflict between his idealism and the stark realities he confronts. Taking a breath to regain his composure, he states, "I comprehend, Pastor Craig. Although these challenges are formidable, I firmly believe that through faith and diligent effort, we can affect meaningful change."

Roger's smile returns, with a hint of skepticism. "Your optimism is admirable, young man. I hope it's enough."

As they continue their discussion, Terrance listens intently, his mind already formulating strategies. He knows the road ahead will be difficult, but he is not deterred. This church, this congregation—they need him. And he needs them. "We'll find a way," Terrance says softly, more to himself than to Roger. "With God's grace, we'll find a way."

As Pastor Roger escorts Terrance from his office, they encounter a woman standing in the hallway, her arms gently crossed over her chest. Her gaze is steady and thoughtful as she looks at Terrance, evaluating him with a hint of curiosity.

"Eleanor Davis," Roger introduced, his voice carrying a note of respect. "Meet Pastor Terrance McAllister." Eleanor narrowed her lips while reaching out her hand, her posture firm and her gaze unwavering. "So you're the new shepherd for our flock," she said, her tone carrying a subtle challenge.

Terrance beamed with warmth as he took her hand gently, his grip firm yet respectful. "It's truly a pleasure to meet you, Eleanor! I can't wait to work together with you and everyone in the congregation."

Eleanor raised an eyebrow, her expression skeptical. "What precisely qualifies you to lead us, young man? Calvary has endured for generations. We require more than mere youthful enthusiasm."

Terrance pushed aside the flicker of uncertainty he felt. He met Eleanor's gaze steadily, his voice calm and sincere. "You're absolutely right, Eleanor. While enthusiasm is wonderful, effective leadership takes more than that. I offer a fresh perspective, rooted in Scripture, and a heartfelt commitment to nurturing our community's spiritual growth. My goal is to honor the traditions that have sustained Calvary while also finding ways to engage and inspire our congregation in new and meaningful ways."

Eleanor is quick with her response. "While your words may sound appealing, what is your strategy for attracting individuals back to these vacant pews? How do you intend to engage those who have distanced themselves from us?"

Terrance took a moment to gather his thoughts before responding to Eleanor's pointed questions. He knew that a clear and actionable plan was essential to gain her trust and the trust of the congregation.

"That's a great question, Eleanor," he began, his tone thoughtful. "First, we need to reconnect with those who have distanced themselves. I propose we start with a series of community listening sessions. These sessions will allow us to hear directly from former and current members about their concerns, needs, and hopes for the church. It's important that we show them we value their input and are committed to addressing their issues."

"Additionally, we can implement outreach programs that meet people where they are. For example, organizing family-friendly events like picnics, movie nights, and community service projects can help us engage with young families and individuals who might feel disconnected. These events can be held both on and off the church campus to reach a broader audience."

"We should also consider enhancing our online presence. Many people today look for community and spiritual guidance online. By improving our website, offering live-streamed services, and engaging on social media, we can reach those who might not be able to attend in person but still want to be part of our community."

"Lastly, we need to revitalize our worship services. While maintaining our cherished traditions, we can introduce elements that resonate with a wider audience. This might include contemporary music alongside our hymns, interactive sermons, and opportunities for congregational participation."

Terrance paused, looking at Eleanor with a determined yet open expression. "These are just a few ideas, and I'm eager to hear more from the congregation. Together, we can create a welcoming and vibrant community that honors our past while embracing the future."

Eleanor's stern expression softened as she listened to Terrance's thoughtful response. She uncrossed her arms and nodded slowly, a hint of a smile forming at the corners of her lips "I must admit, Pastor Terrance, your ideas are well-thought-out and show a genuine understanding of our needs. It's evident, you've invested considerable effort in crafting strategies that honor our traditions while paving the way for progress."

She took a step closer, her tone more encouraging. "I deeply appreciate your willingness to listen and engage with the congregation. It's been a long time since we've had someone so committed to bridging the gap between our past and future."

"I'm eager to see how these strategies unfold and how we can collaborate to revitalize Calvary," she added.

Terrance felt a wave of relief and gratitude wash over him. "Thank you, Eleanor. Your support means a great deal. Together, we can truly make a lasting impact."

Terrance pauses, sensing the warmth beneath her serious demeanor. "It's all about meeting people where they are, Eleanor. We want to show them that God's love isn't confined to these walls; it's vibrant in our actions and how we reach out to others, being the heart, hands, and feet of Jesus."

Eleanor's expression softens. "Those are some bold claims, Pastor! I'm curious to see if you can deliver on them."

Eleanor prepares to exit, her expression now more open and thoughtful. As she turns to leave, a tall gentleman with salt-and-pepper hair approaches her, his countenance marked with concern. "Henry Jenkins," he states with formality, extending his hand to Terrance. "Chair of the Finance Committee."

Terrance's stomach tightens as he recollects Roger's previous cautions concerning the financial condition of the church. He shakes Henry's hand, trying to mask his apprehension with a polite smile. "Nice to meet you, Mr. Jenkins."

Henry gestures toward a nearby office, his tone serious. "If you have a moment, Pastor, we need to discuss some figures."

Terrance nods, feeling the weight of the situation. "Of course, let's talk."

As they walk towards the office, Eleanor gives Terrance a reassuring nod. "Good luck, Pastor. We'll be rooting for you."

Terrance appreciates the gesture, but his mind is already racing with thoughts of the upcoming conversation. Entering the office, he sees a stack of financial reports on the desk. Henry closes the door behind them and motions for Terrance to sit.

A New Beginning: Arrival in Oakridge

"Pastor," Henry begins, his voice steady but grave, "our financial situation is dire. We've been struggling to meet our expenses, and the decline in attendance has only made things worse. We need to find a way to stabilize our finances and ensure the church's sustainability."

Terrance listens intently, his mind already formulating potential solutions. "I understand, Henry. Let's go through the numbers and see where we can make adjustments. We might need to consider fundraising initiatives, cost-cutting measures, and perhaps even seeking external support. It's going to be challenging, but I'm committed to finding a way forward."

Henry nods, a glimmer of hope in his eyes. "Thank you, Pastor. Your willingness to tackle these issues head-on is encouraging. Let's get started."

As Terrance reviewed the financial reports, a renewed sense of purpose surged within him. Despite the challenges, he steadfastly committed to shepherding Calvary through this difficult time and moving him toward a more promising future.

Closing his eyes briefly, he offered a silent prayer to God. When he reopened them, his spark of determination reignited. "Then that's exactly what we'll strive for, Henry. Together, as a team!" he declared.

Before the weight of Henry's financial report could fully settle in his mind, a knock on the slightly open office door drew his attention. A tall, slender man with a seasoned face of wisdom approached.

"Hello, I'm Merle Thompson," he said warmly, extending his hand to Terrance. Merle's eyes glimmered with optimism, illuminating his otherwise somber demeanor. "I truly hope I'm not interrupting, but I wanted to ensure we welcome our new pastor in the best way possible!"

Merle's gaze shifted to the financial reports scattered across the desk, his expression a mix of concern and understanding. "These are tough times, that's for sure," he said, his voice steady and reassuring. "But I've seen this church overcome challenges before, Pastor Terrance. With a little faith and determination, I'm confident we can navigate this together!"

An inkling of hope flickered within Terrance. "Sounds like you may have been with Calvary for quite a while?"

Merle's chuckle was soft, his eyes twinkling with the weight of countless memories. "Indeed, I have. I've been a member here for over thirty years. I've seen pastors come and go, and I've watched this congregation weather many storms. Each time, we've managed to find our way through with God's grace and the support of our community."

Terrance leaned forward, his curiosity piqued. "That's incredible, Merle. Your experience and insight will be invaluable as we work to revitalize the church. What do you think are the most important steps we should take right now?"

Merle's expression grew contemplative, his hands folding neatly on the desk. "First and foremost, we need to rebuild trust within the congregation. Many members are wary of change, especially after past experiences. We should start by listening to their concerns and showing them that their voices matter. Transparency and open communication will be key."

He paused, his gaze drifting momentarily as if recalling specific instances from the past. "We also need to focus on community engagement. Hosting events that bring people together, both within and outside the church, can help us reconnect with those who have drifted away. And, of course, we must address our financial situation with careful planning and creative solutions."

Terrance nodded, a renewed sense of purpose settling in his chest. "Thank you, Merle. Your advice is spot-on. I'm looking forward to working closely with you and the rest of the congregation to bring new life to Calvary."

Merle's smile was warm, his demeanor exuding quiet confidence. "I'm glad to hear that, Pastor. Together, we'll make a difference. One step at a time."

Terrance feels a strong connection to Merle's wisdom and steadfast faith as their conversation unfolds. At last, he meets someone who appreciates the dance between cherishing tradition and embracing the need for change. "You know," Merle says thoughtfully, "In my years in the corporate world, I learned that the key to navigating change is to bring people along with you—not to push them, but to *invite* them to be part of the journey."

Terrance nods, feeling a surge of gratitude for this unexpected ally. "That's precisely the approach I intend to take, Merle. Thank you for your insights and your warm welcome. It means more than you realize."

Terrance redirects his focus to his sermon notes after Merle leaves, feeling intimidated by the blank page but encouraged by the importance of the moment. Terrance closes his eyes momentarily, praying to heaven for guidance. When he opens them again, he picks up his type on his computer. He decides to focus on the theme of renewal and community, drawing from the challenges and opportunities that lie ahead for Calvary.

A New Beginning: Arrival in Oakridge

"Brothers and sisters," he writes, "we stand at a crossroads, facing both uncertainty and possibility. Our church has a rich history, one that has seen us through many trials. Today, we are called to come together, to listen to one another, and to work hand in hand to build a future that honors our past while embracing new beginnings."

Terrance feels a renewed sense of purpose as the words start to flow. He knows this sermon is just beginning a long journey, but he is ready to lead with faith and courage. With each sentence, he envisions the faces of the congregation, hoping to touch their hearts and ignite a shared vision of Calvary's future.

Sunday morning arrives in the blink of an eye. Terrance finds himself at the pulpit, feeling his heart race as he looks at the small congregation. Despite the nervousness bubbling inside him, he knows God has given him the strength to rise to the occasion and connect with those present. "Lord," he prays silently, "Guide my words. Let them be Your words, Please Jesus, let them see your vision for this church."

Terrance gazes at Beth, seated near the front of the church. She meets his eyes and gives him an encouraging nod, her smile radiating warmth and support. At that moment, Terrance feels renewed purpose wash over him. With a smile, he takes a deep breath and begins. "Dear brothers and sisters in Christ, I'm delighted to stand before you today, not only as your new pastor but also as a fellow traveler on this beautiful journey of faith..."

Terrance's voice grows warmer as he dives deeper into his sermon, his passion growing with each word. "The prophet Isaiah reminds us, *"Behold, I am doing a new thing; now it springs forth, do you not perceive it? I will make a way in the wilderness and rivers in the desert. Isaiah 43:19 (ESV)."*

He takes a moment, his gaze sweeping across the congregation. "Today, we find ourselves at the edge of our own wilderness, but God lovingly promises us hope and renewal."

As Terrance shares his message, he notices the atmosphere change around him. Some congregants lean in, their eyes bright with curiosity. Merle Thompson offers a supportive nod, a gentle smile brightening his face. Meanwhile, Eleanor Davis sits more rigidly in her pew, her arms crossed firmly, her expression doubtful. Undeterred, Terrance continues, "Change can be frightening, but it is through change that we grow. Just as a plant must break through the soil to reach the sun, we too must push beyond our comfort zones to thrive in God's light and fulfill the mission He has entrusted to His Church."

Terrance gestured passionately, his voice resonating throughout the church. "Together, we can revitalize this church. We can be a beacon of hope in Oakridge, reaching out to those who feel lost and alone. We are committed to preserving our traditions and making them relevant and inspiring for everyone who walks through our doors."

He pauses, allowing his words to resonate, then continues with renewed vigor. "God's Word transforms lives, offering solace and support to those in need. We can create a vibrant, welcoming, and loving church by embracing our heritage and future possibilities. Let's work together to build bridges, foster connections, and ensure that every member of our community feels valued and heard."

Terrance's eyes sweep across the congregation, seeing optimism and resilience in their faces. "This is our moment, our opportunity to make a difference. With God's grace and our collective effort, we can turn this church into a sanctuary of hope and renewal. Let's take this journey together, hand in hand, and show Oakridge what it means to be a true community of faith."

As Terrance concludes his sermon, a cautious "Amen" reverberates throughout the congregation. He descends from the pulpit, his heart racing with a combination of exhilaration and anxiety. While engaging in handshakes with departing parishioners, he overhears subdued conversations.

"He seems awfully young, doesn't he?" a gravelly voice mutters.

"I don't know if he has the experience to handle our problems," another whispers.

Despite the murmurs of doubt, a few members of the search committee approach him with more encouraging words.

"Pastor Terrance," says Mrs. Jenkins, a long-time member with a kind smile, "your sermon was heartfelt and inspiring. I believe you have the passion we need to move forward."

Mr. Thompson, another committee member, nods in agreement. "It's clear you care deeply about this community. Your ideas about revitalizing our church are exactly what we need. It won't be easy, but with your leadership, I think we can make real progress."

Ms. Davis, who had been skeptical earlier, steps forward with a thoughtful expression. "You spoke with conviction, Pastor. I appreciate

A New Beginning: Arrival in Oakridge

your willingness to listen and engage with us. It's a good start, and I'm willing to see where this journey takes us."

Terrance feels a wave of relief and gratitude. While there are still doubts to overcome, the support from these key members gives him hope. He smiles warmly, thanking them for their kind words and expressing his eagerness to work together to build a stronger, more vibrant Calvary.

Terrance experiences a tightening sensation in his stomach; however, he persists in maintaining a cordial smile, expressing gratitude to each individual for their attendance. As the final congregant departs, he finds himself in solitude within the sanctuary, the burden of uncertainty settling heavily upon his shoulders.

"Am I genuinely prepared for this undertaking?" he reflects. "Can I truly effect positive change in this context?" The magnitude of the forthcoming challenges appears daunting, nearly overwhelming him. Nevertheless, amidst the ambiguity, his faint ember of determination persists, sustained by his steadfast belief and the flicker of hope he discerned in the eyes of several congregants.

As the sanctuary grows quiet, Beth approaches pushing Grant sleeping in the baby carriage, her presence a comforting anchor. She gently places a hand on his shoulder, her eyes filled with understanding. "You did well, Terrance," she says softly. "I could see how much thought and heart you put into your sermon."

Terrance sighs, his tension easing slightly. "Thank you, Beth. But I can't help but worry about whether I'm truly ready for this. The challenges seem so immense."

Beth smiles reassuringly. "I know it's daunting, but remember, you're not alone in this. You have the support of the congregation, and most importantly, you have faith. We'll take it one step at a time, together."

Terrance nods, feeling a bit more grounded. "You're right. I saw some glimmers of hope today. It's a start."

Beth squeezes his hand gently. "And that's all we need—a start. We'll build from here, and with God's grace, we'll find our way."

Terrance feels a renewed sense of resolve. With Beth by his side and the support of the congregation, he is ready to face the challenges ahead and lead Calvary towards a brighter future.

As they stand together in the quiet sanctuary, Terrance and Beth bow their heads in prayer. "Dear Lord," Terrance begins, his voice steady and heartfelt, "we come before you seeking wisdom, clarity, and a shepherd's heart. Guide us as we embark on this journey to revitalize our church and strengthen our community. Grant us the courage to face the challenges ahead and the grace to lead with compassion and understanding. Amen."

Beth adds softly, "Amen. And may we always remember to lean on You and each other, trusting in Your plan for us and for Calvary."

With their prayer concluded, Terrance feels a profound sense of peace and determination. Together, they step forward, ready to embrace the future with faith and hope.

Recommendation

> The initial stage of a change initiative requires leaders to assess the mission, vision, values, history, and culture. Leaders must act as the primary drivers, creating energy and focus by emphasizing the mission and purpose rather than fear-based motivation. Successful churches clearly articulate the issue, communicate it consistently, and engage members through feedback and dialogue.

Discussion Questions

Initial Impressions and Challenges

1. What were your initial thoughts when you arrived at your church? How did the church's physical state influence your perception of the challenges ahead?

2. How did you handle the transition from the previous pastor? What were some key challenges you faced during this period?

Congregational Dynamics

3. How do you address resistance to change within your congregation? Can you share any strategies that have fostered acceptance and enthusiasm for new initiatives?

4. What steps do you take to build trust with key members of the congregation, especially those who may be skeptical of your leadership?

Financial Management

5. How do you approach financial challenges within the church? What measures have you implemented to improve the church's financial health?
6. How important is transparency in financial matters, and how do you ensure that the congregation is informed and involved in financial decisions?

Personal Resilience and Support

7. Have you ever experienced doubts about your ability to lead? How do you cope with these feelings and maintain your resolve?
8. Who are your key supporters within the church, and how do they help you navigate difficult times?

Sermon Preparation and Delivery

9. Can you describe your experience delivering your first sermon at your current church? How did you prepare, and what emotions did you feel during the service?
10. How do you engage a diverse congregation during your sermons? How do you address varying levels of interest and skepticism?

Long-Term Vision

11. What is your long-term vision for the church? How do you plan to achieve this vision amidst the challenges you face?
12. What legacy do you hope to leave at your church? How do you measure the impact of your leadership on the congregation and the community?

2

Crossroads of Faith: Navigating Tradition and Change

> "Trust in the Lord with all your heart and lean not on your own understanding; in all your ways submit to him, and he will make your paths straight."
> —Proverbs 3:5–6

Recommendation

> The church often resists change. This chapter examines what happens when the irresistible force of change encounters the immovable object of the church's resistance to change. The desired outcome is to equip churches with a successful process for managing change while maintaining interpersonal relationships.

Pastor Terrance McAllister paused at the entrance of the finance committee meeting room, his hand resting on the cool brass doorknob. He took a deep breath, the weight of the moment pressing heavily on him. This was his first meeting as the shepherd of Calvary, and he was acutely aware of the high stakes. The church faced a financial crisis that threatened its very future, and the decisions made tonight could either set it on a path to renewal or deepen its struggles.

The room beyond was dimly lit, the soft glow of overhead lights casting long shadows on walls adorned with framed photographs of past congregational events. The faint hum of conversation seeped through the door, a reminder of the critical discussions awaiting him.

Terrance's mind raced with thoughts of the church's dwindling attendance, the financial struggles, and the urgent need for revitalization. He clutched the stack of notes in his hand, each page filled with meticulously prepared ideas and strategies—potential lifelines for the church. He closed his eyes, sending a silent prayer for wisdom and strength.

As he pushed open the door, the room's occupants turned to face him. The finance committee members, a mix of seasoned veterans and newer faces, greeted him with nods and polite smiles. The air was thick with tension, yet there was an undercurrent of hope, a shared desire to find solutions.

Terrance stepped forward, his voice steady despite the turmoil inside him. "Good evening, everyone," he began. "Thank you for gathering here tonight. We face significant challenges, but I believe that together, we can navigate these difficulties and pave the way for a brighter future for Calvary Church."

With that, he took his seat at the table, determined to lead his congregation through this storm and towards renewal.

As Terrance assumes his position at the head of the table, he observes the diverse range of emotions displayed on the countenances of those surrounding him. Certain individuals, such as Elder John Lucas, show expressions of measured optimism. Conversely, other senior members regard him with subtle skepticism that is difficult to hide. "Lord, grant me the wisdom to bridge these divides," Terrance prays silently.

Elder John Lucas takes a moment to gather himself before calling the meeting to order. "Friends, it's wonderful to see you all here tonight as we come together to discuss the challenges facing our beloved Calvary Church," he begins, his warm hazel eyes embracing everyone in the room. "Before we dive into the financial reports, I want to take a moment to share some heartfelt feedback we received this past Sunday."

Terrance leans forward, his interest piqued. On Sunday, he noticed a young couple with two small children in the congregation, a rare sight in recent months.

John continues, his voice growing softer. "A young family visited us for the first time. They praised the beauty of our church and the warmth of our welcome, but . . ." He pauses, and Terrance notices the conflict in the elder's eyes. "They expressed disappointment about our lack of programs for young families."

A palpable sense of unease permeates the room. Terrance observes as the committee members shift in their seats, exchanging uneasy glances. He can almost hear the unspoken thoughts: Change is needed, but at what cost to our established traditions?

Oliver shares his thoughts passionately, his hands gesturing expressively as he talks. "I really care about this church, and it's important that we acknowledge the changes happening around us. What if we explored some contemporary worship styles? Or launched community outreach programs that resonate with today's needs?"

Eleanor's lips pursed, her brow furrowing. "And abandon everything that makes us who we are?"

"Not abandon," Oliver gently counters. "Evolve. It's like welcoming a new instrument into the orchestra. We can hold on to our core values while discovering exciting new ways to express them."

The room erupts into a flurry of voices, some supporting Oliver's ideas and others voicing concerns. Terrance watches as the committee divides, and the tension in the room is palpable. His heart races, feeling the weight of conflicting viewpoints and the big decision ahead. " How can I possibly navigate this?" " he wonders, noticing his palms growing clammy. The voices around him grow louder and more insistent, leaving Terrance feeling frozen, caught in the tug-of-war between tradition and progress.

As Eleanor's words hang in the air, Oliver Williams leans forward, his eyes bright with enthusiasm. He runs a hand through his tousled hair, unable to contain his excitement. "I totally understand, Eleanor," Oliver replies enthusiastically. "But what if our traditions are actually holding us back? It feels like we're a band that keeps playing the same old song while the world has embraced an exciting new genre!" A few chuckles ripple through the room, and Terrance notices some of the younger committee members nodding in agreement.

Terrance surveys the room, observing how some members nod in agreement with Eleanor, while others shift uncomfortably. He feels the weight of tradition himself, recognizing its comfort during uncertain times. Yet, a quiet voice within him whispers of the need for change and growth. Eleanor reflects thoughtfully, her voice warming a bit. "The Lord has been our guiding light during tough times before. Maybe instead of trying to change who we are, we should focus on recommitting to the values that have always been the heart of Calvary Church."

As Eleanor shares her thoughts, Terrance listens intently, reflecting on her words. "How can we celebrate our rich history while welcoming what's ahead?" he wonders. Though the challenge seems daunting, his optimism persists. Maybe there's a wonderful way to connect our cherished traditions with exciting innovations, creating a path that honors both journeys.

Terrance decides to seize the moment. "This feedback is crucial," he begins, his voice steady. "It's a clear indication that while we have a welcoming community, we need to adapt to meet the needs of young families. This doesn't mean abandoning our traditions, but rather finding ways to enhance them to be more inclusive."

Henry Jenkins, the chair of the finance committee, nods thoughtfully. "Pastor Terrance is right. We need to consider how we can allocate resources to develop programs that will attract and retain young families. This could be an investment in our future."

Merle Thompson, who had been quietly listening, speaks up. "We could start small, perhaps with a few family-oriented events or a Sunday school program. It's about showing that we are responsive to the needs of our community."

Elder John Lucas looks around the room, seeing the tentative nods of agreement. "It seems we are all in agreement that change is necessary. The question now is how we can implement these changes while staying true to our core values."

Terrance feels a surge of positive movement. "Let's form a task force to explore these ideas further. We can gather input from the congregation, especially from families, to ensure that any new programs align with their needs and our mission."

The committee members exchange glances, and one by one, they nod in agreement. John smiles, a sense of relief evident in his eyes. "Thank you, Pastor Terrance. Your leadership is exactly what we need to navigate these challenging times."

John nods thoughtfully, appreciating Terrance' s direct approach. 'That' s a great question, Terrance. I think we need to start by understanding what young families are looking for in a church community. Perhaps we could conduct a survey or hold a few focus groups to gather their input." Mary, another committee member, chimes in, 'I agree with John. We also need to assess our current programs and see which ones can be updated or expanded to be more family- friendly. Maybe we could introduce more activities for children and youth and create spaces where parents can connect and support one another." Terrance smiles, feeling the positive energy in the room. 'Those are excellent suggestions. Let's form a small task force to work on this. We can start by reaching out to families in our congregation and the wider community to get their thoughts. Together, we can create a plan that honors our traditions while embracing new opportunities." The committee members nod in agreement, ready to take on the challenge. The meeting continues with a renewed sense of purpose and optimism as they brainstorm ideas and outline the next steps for revitalizing Calvary Church.

Henry interjects, "What traditions are most important to preserve?" Terrance pauses to reflect on the question. 'That' s a crucial point, and I believe it's important to maintain the traditions that define our identity and values. For instance, our annual community service projects have always been a cornerstone of our outreach efforts. They not only help those in need but also bring our congregation together in a meaningful way." John adds, 'Our music ministry is another tradition that resonates deeply with many members. The choir and instrumental performances have always provided inspiration and joy." Mary nods, 'And let's not forget our holiday celebrations. Events like the Christmas Eve service and Easter sunriseservice are cherished by families and create lasting memories." Terrance smiles, 'Absolutely. These traditions are the heart and soul of Calvary Church. As we move forward, we need to find ways to integrate these beloved practices with new initiatives that appeal to younger families. It's about creating a balance that honors our past while embracing the future." The committee members agree, feeling a renewed sense of purpose as they discuss how to preserve these important traditions while adapting to the changing needs of their community.

"Nehemiah's goal was not just to rebuild physical walls; he also aimed to restore faith and hope in a community facing great hardship," Terrance continues. In the same vein, we must rebuild and renew our church to create an environment where everyone feels welcome and supported."

He opens his Bible to Nehemiah 4:14 and reads aloud: "After I looked things over, I stood up and said to the nobles, the officials and the rest of the people, 'Don't be afraid of them. Remember the Lord, who is great and awesome, and fight for your families, your sons and your daughters, your wives and your homes.'"

Terrance looks up, meeting the eyes of each committee member. "Just as Nehemiah encouraged his people to persevere and fight for their community, we too must stand strong and work together. Our mission is not just to preserve our traditions, but to adapt and grow, ensuring that Calvary Church remains a beacon of hope for generations to come."

The room fills with a renewed sense of purpose and determination. The committee members nod in agreement, ready to embrace the challenge ahead and bring new life to their beloved church.

Henry Jenkins stands from his chair, his formidable stature casting a shadow across the table. The room falls into silence as he clears his throat, his penetrating blue eyes surveying the faces of the committee members. Terrance experiences the gravity of Henry's presence, a blend of respect and apprehension settling in his chest. "Brothers and sisters," Henry begins, his deep voice resonating throughout the room, "I'm afraid the numbers don't paint a pretty picture. Our membership has declined by fifteen percent over the past year, and our weekly offerings are down by nearly a quarter."

Terrance observes the committee members' expressions grow somber. Sarah Thompson's shoulders droop, while Robert Chen's typically jovial countenance shifts to one of concern. "If this trend continues," Henry proceeds, "we'll be facing some difficult decisions in the coming months. We may need to consider cutting programs or even reducing staff hours." A collective intake of breath fills the room.

Terrance feels the weight of Henry's words, but he knows this moment is crucial. He stands up, his voice steady and filled with resolve. "Thank you, Henry, for bringing these issues to our attention. While the numbers are indeed concerning, I believe this is also an opportunity for us to come together and find creative solutions. We have faced challenges before, and with God's guidance, we have always found a way through."

He looks around the room, making eye contact with each committee member. "Let's not see this as a setback, but as a call to action. We need to engage our congregation more deeply, reach out to those who have drifted away, and find new ways to connect with our community. Together, we can turn this situation around."

A sense of determination begins to replace the initial shock. Sarah straightens her shoulders, and Robert's expression softens with a hint of optimism. The committee members nod, ready to tackle the challenges ahead with renewed vigor and faith.

Terrance's mind swirls with doubt. He wonders if he is truly equipped to lead the congregation through such turbulent times. The weight of his calling feels heavier than ever, and he questions whether he has the strength to carry it. Will these financial concerns end his ministry at Calvary?

Terrance notices Eleanor Davis straightening in her chair, her lips pressed into a thin line. Before he can speak, she rises, her voice cutting through the anxious whispers. "While I appreciate Henry's thorough report," Eleanor commences, "I feel compelled to remind everyone of the significance of remaining faithful to our foundational principles." Her gaze, typically unwavering, now reveals a blend of resolve and apprehension. "Our traditions have sustained this church through generations. We must not forsake them at the first indication of adversity."

As Eleanor speaks, her words resonate deeply with him. He knows she is right; their traditions are the bedrock of their community. Yet, he can't shake the fear that they might not be enough to overcome the current challenges.

Taking a deep breath, Terrance rises to address the committee. "Thank you, Eleanor, for reminding us of the importance of our traditions. They are indeed the foundation upon which we stand. But I must confess, I am struggling with the enormity of the task before us. How can we honor our past while ensuring a future for Calvary Church?"

The room falls silent, committee members sensing Terrance's vulnerability. Sarah Thompson speaks up, her tone gentle but firm. "Pastor Terrance, your leadership will be a source of strength for us. We believe in you and our collective ability to navigate these challenges. We are here to support you, just as you have supported us."

Robert Chen nods in agreement. "We need to trust in our faith and in each other. Together, we can find a way to balance our traditions with the necessary changes to attract and retain young families."

Terrance feels an inkling of hope. His congregation and committee support give him the courage to face his doubts. "Thank you, Sarah and Robert. Your words mean a lot to me. Let's move forward with faith and determination, knowing we are not alone in this journey."

The committee members nod, their spirits lifted by the renewed sense of unity and purpose. Terrance feels renewed resolve, ready to lead Calvary Church through the challenges ahead.

The next step I suggest in moving forward for Calvary Church is to form a task force dedicated to engaging with young families in our community. Our church can conduct surveys and hold focus groups to better understand what our community wants and needs."

He pauses, ensuring everyone is following. "Second, we should review our current programs and identify opportunities to make them more family-friendly. This might include introducing new activities for children and youth and creating spaces for parents to connect and support each other."

As Terrance scanned the room, he sensed a sense of community. "Finally, let's commit to regular communication with our congregation. Keeping everyone informed and involved will be crucial as we navigate these changes. Together, we can honor our traditions while embracing new opportunities."

The committee members nod in agreement, ready to take on the challenge. As the meeting concludes, Terrance feels a renewed sense of mission, confident that they can bring new life to Calvary Church with the committee's and the congregation's support.

As the meeting concludes, Terrance feels a mix of hope and uncertainty. He notices Eleanor's quiet demeanor and the conflict in her eyes, a reminder of the challenges that lie ahead. The committee members disperse, chatting animatedly about potential changes and next steps.

Terrance heads home to discuss the meeting's events with Beth, his trusted confidante and ministry partner. "Beth, what do you think of today's discussion and plan moving forward?" he asks, seeking her perspective.

Beth smiles warmly, her eyes reflecting the same determination that Terrance feels. "It sounds like it was a productive meeting, Terrance. We have a lot of work ahead, but the committee's willingness to engage and find solutions is encouraging. We must maintain that momentum and ensure everyone feels involved in the process."

Terrance nods, appreciating Beth's insight. "You're right. We need to focus on preserving our traditions while embracing new opportunities. With the committee's and our congregation's support, I believe we can navigate these challenges."

Beth places a reassuring hand on Terrance's shoulder. "We'll get through this together, Terrance. Let's continue to pray for guidance and strength."

Terrance feels a renewed sense of accomplishment as they turn in for the night. The path ahead may be difficult, but with the support of Beth, the committee, and the congregation, he is confident they can bring new life to Calvary Church.

Recommendation

Often, church members overlook the need for change because they fail to recognize the reality of the situation. Many ignore signs of decline, such as decreasing attendance, deteriorating facilities, and diminished outreach effectiveness. This lack of awareness often arises from a strong attachment to tradition and reluctance to admit that current methods may no longer be effective.

As a leader, guide the congregation in facing this reality. Clearly communicate challenges like financial struggles, facility repairs, and the need to revitalize outreach. Present these issues honestly yet optimistically, emphasizing that acknowledging them is the first step toward solutions.

Instill a sense of urgency by helping the congregation understand that without proactive efforts, the church's future is at risk. Encourage them to view change as a necessary evolution to preserve and strengthen the church's mission. Foster a collective sense of responsibility to inspire action and revitalize the church's impact on the community.

Discussion Questions

When navigating change, prioritize building trust in your relationships with key stakeholders. Consider the way Pastor Terrance listened to his committee members. How did his initial interactions with the finance committee set the tone for his leadership? What can we learn?

Initial Impressions and Leadership Challenges

1. How did Pastor Terrance's initial interactions with the finance committee establish the tone for his leadership? What can we learn from his approach to stepping into a new leadership role?
2. How important is it for a new leader to understand the existing dynamics and challenges of a congregation? What strategies can be used to navigate this transition smoothly?

CROSSROADS OF FAITH: NAVIGATING TRADITION AND CHANGE

Financial and Membership Concerns

3. How can church leaders address financial struggles and declining membership in a way that is transparent and constructive?

4. Church leaders should address financial struggles and declining membership by openly communicating the challenges, engaging the congregation in brainstorming solutions, and implementing strategic plans that balance transparency, community involvement, and faith-based initiatives.

5. What steps can be taken to attract and retain young families in the congregation? How can programs be developed to meet their needs without alienating other members?

Balancing Tradition and Innovation

6. How can church leaders balance the preservation of traditions with the adoption of change and innovation? What are the potential risks and benefits associated with each approach?

7. How can leaders facilitate productive discussions when there are strong opposing views within the committee or congregation?

Personal Resilience and Support

8. How can leaders manage their feelings of doubt and overwhelm when confronted with significant challenges? What role does faith play in fostering resilience?

9. How important is it for leaders to have trusted advisors or mentors like Merle Thompson? How can these relationships be cultivated and maintained?

Scriptural Guidance and Reflection

10. How can scriptural references, like the story of Nehemiah, be used to inspire and guide a congregation through difficult times? What other Biblical stories might offer similar guidance?

11. How effective are moments of reflection and prayer in calming tensions and refocusing a group's energy? Can you share an example from your own experience?

Long-Term Vision and Collaboration

12. How can leaders communicate a clear and compelling vision for the future that fosters open-mindedness and collaboration?
13. What strategies can be employed to win the support of skeptical members like Eleanor Davis? How can leaders demonstrate the value of new ideas while respecting existing traditions?

Personal Reflections and Next Steps

14. How do you balance honoring tradition while embracing necessary transformation in your leadership role?
15. What are your hopes and plans for the future of your congregation? How do you plan to address the challenges and opportunities that lie ahead?

3

A Voice of Wisdom: The Search for a Mentor

*"Don't wait until the conditions are perfect to start.
Starting makes the conditions perfect."*

Keys to Find a Christian Mentor/Coach

> Finding a Christian mentor or coach who is spiritually mature and has a strong personal relationship with Jesus Christ is crucial. Identify a mentor with experience and wisdom in the areas you wish to grow in, who communicates effectively and offers encouraging support. A genuine passion for discipleship, commitment, and consistency is indispensable. Make sure your mentor shares your faith and values, provides accountability, and provides emotional support. Their experiences can offer practical insights to help you apply biblical principles to daily life, fostering spiritual and personal growth.

Terrance stands in the heart of his cluttered office, where the floor is a delightful tangle of papers. His eyes dance from the stacks of unopened mail to the books perched precariously on the edge of a well-loved desk, finally landing on the clock that ticks cheerfully on the wall. He wraps his fingers around his phone, holding it close as if that could strengthen the connection to the friendly voice on the other end.

"Kevin, it's been too long," Terrance says, a smile spreading across his face as he hears the familiar voice of his seminary friend.

"Terrance! It sure has. How have you been, my friend?" Kevin Lewis' voice is warm and full of genuine curiosity.

Terrance leans back in his chair, feeling a wave of nostalgia wash over him. "It's been a challenging season, Kevin. Our church is facing some tough times, and I've been questioning my ability to lead through it."

Kevin's tone shifts to one of concern. "I'm sorry to hear that, Terrance. But remember, you're not alone in this. Sometimes, reconnecting with old friends can bring new perspectives. Let's talk through it. What's been going on?"

Terrance shares with Kevin Calvary's financial struggles and the resistance he has experienced from some of the older members. "It's been tough, Kevin. The financial situation is dire, and some of the older members are resistant to change. They hold our traditions dear, which I understand, but it's making it hard to move forward."

Kevin listens intently and asks, "Do you have anyone who can serve as a mentor and offer guidance and support during this time?"

Terrance pauses, recalling a recent conversation. "Actually, yes. Merle, a retired CEO, offered to mentor me. He has faced similar challenges in his secular career at a Fortune 500 company and possesses a wealth of experience."

Kevin's voice brightens. "That's great to hear, Terrance. Having a mentor like Merle could be incredibly valuable. He can provide perspective and advice that might help you navigate these difficulties."

Terrance nods, feeling relieved. "You're right, Kevin. I think it's time I took Merle up on his offer. Thank you for reminding me of the importance of seeking support."

Kevin chuckled. "Anytime, my friend. Remember, you're not alone in this. Lean on those who care about you and trust your leadership ability. You've got this."

As the conversation flows, Kevin inquires about Terrance's family. Just hearing the names "Beth" and "little Grant" lights up Terrance's face with a smile. "Beth's just wonderful," Terrance says, "and Grant is growing up so quickly. He's already on his feet, taking his first steps!"

Kevin chuckles warmly. "That's fantastic, Terrance! I remember when my kids were that age. It's such a magical time, watching them discover the world around them. How's Beth handling everything?"

Terrance's smile widens. "She's amazing, Kevin. Balancing her work and taking care of Grant, she's been a rock for our family. I don't know how she does it all with such grace."

A Voice of Wisdom: The Search for a Mentor

Kevin's voice softens with admiration. "Beth sounds like a true partner. It's wonderful to hear that you have such strong support at home. And Grant, taking his first steps—that's a milestone worth celebrating! How are you managing to find time for family amidst all the church challenges?"

Terrance sighs, but his tone remains positive. "It's a juggling act, for sure. But we've made it a priority to spend quality time together, even if it's just a few moments each day. Beth and Grant are my grounding force, reminding me of what's truly important."

Kevin nods, though Terrance can't see it. "That's crucial, Terrance. Family is everything. Make sure to cherish those moments. They can provide the strength you need to face the challenges at Calvary."

Terrance feels a wave of gratitude. "Thanks, Kevin. Your words mean a lot. It's goLet's keep in touch more often."

"Absolutely, Terrance. I'm always here for you.

"Enjoy these moments," Kevin advises, a touch of wistfulness in his tone. "They go by in a blink."

The brief detour into personal matters deepens their bond, making the advice that follows even more impactful. Kevin returns to the topic at hand, his voice unwavering. "Remember, Terrance, we're both serving the same mission. You're never alone in this."

Terrance felt the weight of Kevin's words - their friendship strengthened their bond. "Thanks, Kevin. Your support means a lot. I believe it's time to take the next step and reach out to Merle."

Kevin's voice is encouraging. "That's a great idea, Terrance. Merle's experience will be invaluable. And while you're at it, consider forming a transition team. Having a group dedicated to navigating these changes can make a significant difference."

Terrance nods. "You're right. A transition team can help us manage the challenges and ensure we're moving forward constructively. I'll start by reaching out to Merle and then gather a few key members to form the team."

Kevin's tone is reassuring. "That sounds like a solid plan. Remember, Terrance, you're not alone in this. We're all working towards the same mission, and with the right support, you'll lead Calvary Church through these changes."

Terrance smiles, feeling the strength of their shared mission. "Thanks, Kevin. I'll keep you updated on our progress. Your advice has been incredibly helpful."

"Anytime, Terrance. Take care and send my best to Beth and Grant."

As the call ends, Terrance feels a renewed sense of determination. He picks up his phone again, ready to reach out to Merle and start building the transition team that will help guide Calvary Church toward a brighter future.

Terrance takes a deep breath as he prepares to contact Merle and establish the transition team. He understands that the success of this initiative will rely on the qualities and dedication of the team members.

Recommendation

Similar to Terrance, church leaders navigating change should consider forming a core team with people that have a combination of the following qualities:

1. **Commitment to the Church's Mission:** Team members should be deeply committed to Calvary Church's mission and values, genuinely desiring to see the church thrive.
2. **Open-mindedness:** It's crucial to have individuals who are open to new ideas and willing to embrace change, all while respecting the church's traditions.
3. **Diverse Perspectives:** A team with diverse backgrounds and experiences can provide a well-rounded approach to problem-solving and innovation.
4. **Strong Communication Skills:** Effective communication is key to ensuring that all voices are heard and that the team can work together collaboratively.
5. **Leadership and Initiative:** Members who can take initiative and lead projects will be essential in driving the transition forward.
6. **Empathy and Understanding:** The ability to empathize with various viewpoints and understand the concerns of the congregation will aid in making thoughtful and inclusive decisions.
7. **Problem-solving Abilities:** Creative and strategic thinkers who can develop practical solutions to the challenges the church faces.
8. **Faith and Resilience:** A strong faith and the resilience to persevere through difficult times will be vital for maintaining morale and focus.

A Voice of Wisdom: The Search for a Mentor

Terrance picks up his phone and dials Merle's number, ready to take the first steps in building a brighter future for Calvary Church.

Terrance steps into Merle's pristine and organized home office, feeling a stark contrast to his own cluttered workspace. The tall, slender figure of Merle, dressed in a neatly pressed shirt, enters the study with an air of calm and confidence. Merle looks right at home among the shelves of books and sepia-toned photographs, which crowd the walls like faithful parishioners, bearing witness to years of worship and work.

Terrance settles into the armchair, feeling the comfort of the leather and the warmth of Merle's presence. "Thank you for meeting with me, Merle. Your guidance means a lot, especially during these challenging times."

Merle smiles, his eyes reflecting years of wisdom. "I'm glad you reached out, Terrance. Let's talk about how we can navigate these changes together. What are your thoughts on what's next?" In a conversation with a seminary friend, he suggested I form a transition team. What are your thoughts on forming a transition team?

Merle leans forward, eager to share his ideas. "I believe a transition team is essential. We need members who are committed to our mission, open-minded, and proficient in strong communication. They should bring diverse perspectives and have the ability to empathize with the concerns of our " congregation."

Terrance nods in agreement. "Those are excellent qualities to look for. It's important to have a team that can balance tradition with innovation." Merle, you know the folks here; I need your help to identify potential members who embody these traits."

As they continue their discussion, Terrance feels his confidence growing. With Merle's mentorship and the support of a dedicated transition team, he is assured that they can guide Calvary Church toward a brighter future.

Merle leaned back in his chair, thinking. "Terrance, as we move forward, anticipating challenges is imperative. Change is never easy, and there will be resistance, especially from those who hold our traditions dear."

Terrance nodded, feeling Merle's weight. "I understand. Some of our older members have already expressed concerns. How do we address their fears while still pushing for necessary changes?"

Merle smiled gently. "It's about balance and communication. We need to reassure them that our traditions will not be lost but rather integrated into a new vision for the future. Regular updates and open forums where they can voice their concerns will be crucial."

Terrance felt a sense of clarity. "That makes sense. We also need to be prepared for financial challenges. Our resources are limited, and we must find ways to engage the congregation in supporting our initiatives."

Merle nodded. "Indeed. Transparency about our financial situation and involving the congregation in brainstorming solutions can foster ownership and commitment. Additionally, exploring new fundraising opportunities and partnerships can help bridge the gap."

Terrance's confidence grows with each passing moment. "Thank you, Merle. Your insights are invaluable. With your mentorship and the support of a dedicated transition team, I believe we can guide Calvary Church."

Merle's eyes twinkle with encouragement. "Remember, Terrance, you're not alone in this. Lean on your team, your congregation, and your faith. Together, we can overcome any challenge."

As they conclude their discussion, Terrance gains more clarity on his purpose and determination. With Merle's guidance and the collective effort of the transition team, he is ready to lead Calvary Church through the challenges ahead and into a new era of growth and renewal.

Terrance receives Merle's advice like water from a deep well, finding it refreshing and plentiful. Merle offers concrete examples from his days in the corporate world, illustrating the need for strategic planning. "You monitor change," he says, tapping a pencil against the desk, "by looking at what it accomplishes, not just how it begins." Terrance takes in each word, his mind soaking up Merle's insights.

Merle chuckles. "That's how I felt the day I took my first job," he shares. "Excitement and fear are two sides of the same coin, young man." Terrance asks questions, leaning forward, eyes bright with anticipation. Merle answers with the patience of one who has walked the path before, each response crafted with care and clarity.

Terrance feels supported by Merle's words, which reassure him that the past and future can coexist. He shares his vision for the church, which includes elders, youth, tradition, and innovation—bringing fresh dynamics to worship, creating children's programming, and planning community events. He wants Calvary to define itself as a Christ-proclaiming congregation that serves as a light to the community.

"Be bold," Merle advises. "But be patient. Change doesn't happen overnight. Sometimes, the quietest progress is the most profound."

A Voice of Wisdom: The Search for a Mentor

Merle's wisdom settles over him. He sees that the path is not as daunting, and mentors like Merle make it easier.

They discussed potential obstacles. The conversation turned to resistance.

"Address concerns directly," Merle suggested. "People fear what they don't understand. You can have brilliant strategies, but if you can't communicate them, your ideas won't succeed."

Terrance nodded thoughtfully. "You're right. Communication is key. We need to ensure everyone understands the vision and feels included in the process."

Merle continues, "Exactly. It's about being transparent and being open. If we can explain our strategies clearly and address misconceptions, we can reduce resistance."

Terrance added, "And we should also be receptive to feedback. Sometimes, resistance comes from valid concerns that we might have overlooked."

Merle smiles. "That's true. By engaging in an open dialogue, we can turn potential obstacles into growth opportunities. It's a collaborative effort. So, let's ensure our communication is clear, direct, and inclusive. That way, we can navigate resistance effectively and move forward together."

Terrance nods, absorbing the lesson with renewed purpose. He knows the task ahead is a marathon, not a sprint, and he's prepared to run the distance. He expresses his gratitude. "You've given me a lot to think about," he says, repeating some key advice to show his understanding. "I can't thank you enough for your guidance."

Merle smiled warmly, seeing Terrance's determination. "Remember, you're not alone on this journey. Lean on your community, seek support from your peers, and trust in the process. Every step you take, no matter how small, brings you closer to your vision."

Terrance felt a wave of reassurance wash over him. "I'll keep that in mind. It's comforting to know I have people like you to turn to."

Merle's wisdom settles over him, making the path ahead seem less daunting. With mentors like Merle by his side, Terrance feels ready to face the challenges and embrace the opportunities ahead.

Merle adds, "Think of your vision like a garden." Seeds take time to grow into strong, flourishing plants. With patience, care, and nurturing, you'll see your efforts bloom into something beautiful and lasting."

Terrance smiles, inspired by the metaphor. "That's a wonderful way to look at it. I'll nurture this vision with all the care it deserves."

Terrance nods, absorbing the lessons. He knows now that the task ahead is a marathon, not a sprint, and he's prepared to run the distance.

"It's a pleasure," Merle replies, his simple words masking the depth of his commitment. "Remember, Terrance, you're part of something bigger than any one of us."

The conversation wraps up with a sense of completion, both men aware of the significance of their exchange. Terrance stands, the study's history enveloping him like an embrace as he prepares to leave. As he exits, Terrance is filled with determination, the weight of tradition no longer a burden but a foundation. Now is the time to begin to put the plan to paper.

As Terrance steps out of the study, the sense of completion from their conversation lingers, both men acutely aware of its significance. The history of the room seems to embrace him, transforming the weight of tradition into a solid foundation for his newfound determination. Now is the time to begin putting the plan to paper. However, one evening, after a particularly challenging day, Terrance finds himself alone in his office, exhausted and overwhelmed. Plans for children's programs have hit a snag; some congregation members oppose his changes. He feels their skepticism and wonders if he's pushing too aggressively, too fast. He gazed out the window. The metaphor for gardens feels distant and unattainable. Doubt creeps in, whispering that perhaps his vision is too ambitious, that he might not be able to bridge the gap between tradition and innovation. Fear of failure looms large, and for a moment, he considers scaling back his plans. But then he remembered Merle's words about patience and quiet progress. He takes a deep breath, reminding himself that growth takes time and setbacks are a part of the journey. He reaches out to Merle and Kevin for advice, knowing their support can help him navigate these challenges. Terrance feels renewed optimism. He understands that doubt is natural, but doesn't have to derail his vision. With patience, care, and the right nurturing, he believes he can overcome these obstacles and see his efforts bloom into something beautiful and lasting.

The next day, Terrance met with Merle to discuss his concerns. He expressed his doubts and challenges. Merle listened attentively, nodding as Terrance spoke.

"Terrance, it's completely normal to feel overwhelmed," Merle said gently. "Every aspiring vision encounters obstacles. The key is to stay focused on your goals and remember why you started this journey.

A Voice of Wisdom: The Search for a Mentor

Terrance feels more at ease as Merle continues. "Think of these challenges as opportunities to refine your approach. Each setback is a chance to learn and grow. You're doing meaningful work, and it's okay to take things one step at a time."

Merle's words resonate deeply with Terrance. "Thank you, Merle. Your support means a lot to me. I'll keep pushing forward, knowing that progress, even if slow, is still progress.

Merle smiled warmly. "You're on the right path, Terrance. Keep nurturing your vision with patience and care. You'll see it flourish in ways you never imagined.

Merle adds, "Start by reaching out to congregation members like Eleanor. She's been a pillar of support for many years and has a wealth of experience. Her insights and encouragement can be invaluable as you navigate through these changes. Terrance nods. "That's an awesome idea. Eleanor's wisdom and perspective will be helpful. I'll reach out to her and other key members to build a strong foundation for our vision.

Terrance feels ready to face the challenges ahead, knowing he has the support and wisdom of mentors like Merle and the valuable insights of congregation members like Eleanor to guide him."

Terrance sat across from Eleanor in his home office, with Beth and Grant in the other room, their conversation heavy in the air. He appreciated Eleanor's willingness to join him, knowing her insights were invaluable. Yet, as she spoke, he could sense tension in her voice.

"I'm honored to be included, Pastor Terrance," Eleanor said, with a tone respectful but tinged with concern. "However, I'm very worried. Our direction seems to be leading the congregation towards another painful split."

Terrance nodded, understanding the gravity of her words. "I understand your concerns, Eleanor. This is a challenging time for all of us, and the last thing I want is to cause more division. Can you share more about what specifically worries you?"

Eleanor took a deep breath, her eyes reflecting the turmoil within. "It's the changes you're proposing. While I see the potential benefits, I'm worried that not everyone will be on board. We've been through so much already, and I'm afraid this might push some members away."

Terrance leaned forward, his expression earnest. "Your concern is valid, and it's something I've been thinking about deeply. My goal is to strengthen our community, not divide it further. I believe with careful planning and open communication, we can navigate these changes together."

Eleanor's gaze softened slightly, but her worry remained. "I hope so, Pastor. But the new worship style you're suggesting is quite different from what we're used to. Many members cherish traditional hymns and might resist contemporary music."

Terrance sighed, acknowledging the challenge. "I understand the attachment to our traditions, Eleanor. However, incorporating contemporary music could attract younger families and help us grow. We can find a balance that respects our heritage while embracing new elements."

Eleanor shook her head slightly, her concern growing. "And what about the children's programs? The changes seem too ambitious. We have always maintained a straightforward, functional approach. I'm worried that these new plans might overwhelm our volunteers and limited resources."

Terrance's determination didn't waver. "The children's programs are crucial to our future. Enhancing them will provide our kids with better engagement and spiritual growth. We can start small and gradually build up, ensuring we have the support and resources needed."

Eleanor's voice grew more urgent. "Lastly, the aggressive community outreach. It's a noble idea, but I'm concerned about the strain it might put on our congregation. We barely have enough people to head our existing ministries and committees; how can we ask the faithful few to wear more hats? We've always been a close-knit community, and this might stretch us too thin."

Terrance met her gaze, his resolve firm. "Community outreach is essential to our mission. It can bring new life and purpose to our congregation. We can approach it strategically, ensuring we don't overextend ourselves while making a meaningful impact."

Eleanor sighed, her worry still evident. "I hope you're right, Pastor. It's just that the wounds of the last split are still fresh for many. We need to proceed with caution and sensitivity."

Terrance nodded, his expression thoughtful. "Absolutely. I plan to involve more members in decision-making and ensure everyone's voice is heard. Your feedback is crucial here, Eleanor. How can we better address these concerns?"

Eleanor's eyes softened, her voice more hopeful. "Perhaps more town hall meetings or small group discussions where people can express their thoughts and feelings openly. Transparency and inclusivity will be key."

Terrance smiled, grateful for her input. "That's a great idea. I'll make sure we implement more opportunities for open dialogue. Thank you for your honesty and support, Eleanor. Together, we can find a path that honors our past and builds a stronger future."

As Eleanor left the study, Terrance realized that more planning and coaching are needed to move forward. After Beth put Grant to bed, she joined Terrance in the living room, where he was still reflecting on his conversation with Eleanor. The room was quiet, the only sound being the soft ticking of the grandfather's clock in the background.

Beth sat down beside Terrance, sensing his weight. "How did the meeting with Eleanor go?" she asked gently.

Terrance sighed, with gratitude and concern in his eyes. "It was intense." Eleanor fears the proposed changes might lead to another painful split in the congregation. She raised valid points about worship style, children's programming, and community outreach."

Beth nodded, understanding the complexity of the situation. "She's right to be concerned. We've seen how quickly things can unravel if we're not careful. What do you think we should do?"

Terrance leaned back, his mind racing with possibilities. "We need to gather a core team of supporters who believe in the vision and can help us navigate these changes. Eleanor suggested more town hall meetings and small group discussions to ensure transparency and inclusivity."

Beth smiled, her support unwavering. "That's an excellent idea. We need to make sure everyone feels heard and involved. It will take time, but it's worth it."

Terrance felt affirmed as he looked at Beth. "You're right. With careful planning and dedicated team support, we can move forward without more division. Eleanor's feedback was invaluable, and we need to build on that."

Beth squeezed his hand, offering her encouragement. "We'll get through this together. Let's start by identifying potential team members and setting up those meetings."

Terrance nodded, feeling more confident. "Thank you, Beth. Your support means everything. Let's make this happen."

As the evening drew to a close, Terrance realized that more planning and coaching were essential to moving forward. With Beth by his side and Eleanor's insights, he felt ready to face the challenges ahead, knowing that together, they could build a stronger future for their congregation.

Discussion Questions

Seeking Support and Mentorship

1. How valuable is it for church leaders to have trusted confidants like Kevin Lewis? What qualities should leaders look for in a coach/mentor?

2. How can seeking mentorship from experienced members within the congregation, like Merle Thompson, benefit new leaders? What are some effective ways to approach potential mentors?

Balancing Tradition and Change

3. How can leaders find a balance between the wisdom of experienced members and the need for innovation and change? What role do personal anecdotes and historical context play in navigating this balance?

4. How can leaders identify and utilize breakthrough moments to inspire change within their congregation?

Personal Resilience and Support

5. How can leaders address their doubts and fears when confronted with significant challenges? What role does faith have in fostering resilience?

6. How important is it for leaders to have a support system within the church? How can these relationships be developed and sustained?

Vision and Optimism

7. How can leaders express a clear and inspiring vision for the future that promotes optimism and collaboration?

8. How should leaders manage opposition from congregation members, like Eleanor Davis? What strategies can be used to address skepticism and resistance?

Reflection and Perseverance

9. What practices can support maintaining a positive outlook and determination?
10. How can leaders prepare for the ongoing transformation journey within their church? What steps can be taken to ensure ongoing growth and improvement?

4

Building Bridges: Forming the Core Team

"Team building is working together to achieve a common goal. It directs individual accomplishments toward organizational objectives. It fuels ordinary people to achieve extraordinary results."

Recruit a Diverse Team

> A clear set of shared values and a mission are essential to building a strong team culture. This is critical at this stage of organizational change. Key stakeholders and influencers must support sustainable change. Transformative leaders excel at sustaining change. An effective coalition must offer strategic authority, capability, credibility, and influence.

Pastor Terrance McAllister stands on the Mitchells' porch, his hand poised to knock. The faint aroma of baking apples wafts through the air, stirring memories of Sunday potlucks and warm fellowship. He takes a deep breath, silently praying for wisdom and grace. The door swings open, revealing Carolyn's beaming face. "Pastor Terrance! Come in, come in." Her gentle voice wraps around him like a blanket.

"Thank you, Carolyn," Terrance says, stepping into the cozy foyer. Jonathan appears from the living room, his quiet strength a steady presence.

Building Bridges: Forming the Core Team

"It's good to see you, Pastor," Jonathan says, clasping Terrance's hand firmly.

As they nestle into the living room, Terrance feels a warm connection to the family photos that grace the walls. Each picture tells a story about the Mitchells' deep ties to the community and their cherished church. There's a comforting sense of tradition that softly fills the air, perfectly blended with the delightful aroma of freshly baked apple pie. Carolyn leans forward, her eyes sparkling with sincerity. "Pastor, the church holds such a special place in our hearts. We've been proud members for over thirty years!" She takes a moment, thoughtfully selecting her words. "These changes you're proposing... they seem to be happening so quickly. I'm a bit concerned we might forget who we are as a community."

Terrance nods, feeling a tug at his servant's heart from the concern in her voice. He wishes to comfort her and share his dream of a lively and flourishing congregation. Yet, he recognizes the importance of listening first. Jonathan clears his throat gently. "I acknowledge Carolyn's concerns," he articulates, his tone deliberate and contemplative. "However, I also observe the empty pews on Sundays. Our community is changing, and maybe . . . maybe we need to change with it." Terrance feels a warm spark of hope at Jonathan's encouraging words. He quietly expresses gratitude to God for this beautiful moment of connection, this lovely bridge linking his cherished past to the bright future he dreams of.

"I appreciate both of your perspectives," Terrance says, leaning forward slightly. "Your voices, your experiences—they're invaluable as we navigate this journey together."

As the conversation continues, Terrance marvels at the delicate balance before him. How can he honor Calvary Church's rich history while also embracing the necessary changes for its future? The challenge seems daunting, but in this moment, surrounded by the warmth of the Mitchells' home and the aroma of freshly baked pie, he feels a renewed sense of purpose and determination. Terrance leans back in his chair, his eyes filled with warmth and understanding. He takes a deep breath, feeling the weight of their concerns and the responsibility of his role. "You know," he begins, his voice soft yet brimming with passion, "it reminds me of the Israelites' journey through the wilderness. They faced uncertainty and fear, but throughout it all, God was right there with them, guiding them toward a bright and promised future."

He pauses, noticing Carolyn's eyes widen slightly at the biblical reference. Terrance continues, "Like them, we're on a journey. It might feel uncomfortable at times, but I believe God is guiding us toward something beautiful." Jonathan nods in understanding while Terrance gazes at Carolyn, his voice gentle. "Carolyn, your concerns are not only valid—they're essential. Your commitment and deep love for this church are the foundation upon which we're building together." Carolyn gently relaxes her shoulders, encouraging Terrance.

He prays, "Lord, help me connect with them and show that change doesn't mean losing our true selves; it's all about building on the foundation to help us flourish together."

Terrance assures with a warm smile, glancing between Carolyn and Jonathan, "I promise you, we're in this together every step of the way. Your wisdom and experience are priceless in shaping the future of Calvary." Carolyn stands up from her seat, her smile lighting up the room. "You know, speaking of tradition," she says, "I believe it's time for some pie!"

The scent of cinnamon and apples fills the room as Carolyn returns with the freshly baked pie. Terrance's mouth waters, and he can't help but smile. This, he thinks, is what it's all about—fellowship, warmth, and tradition. Terrance savors the first bite, closing his eyes in appreciation. "Mrs. Mitchell," he says, "this pie is absolutely heavenly."

Carolyn beams, her earlier tension seeming to melt away. "It's my grandmother's recipe," she explains. "I've been baking it for church potlucks for years." Terrance nods, feeling a wave of insight as he realizes the deeper meaning of this moment. This pie, a beloved recipe handed down through the years, embodies what they're talking about—celebrating the past while looking forward to the future.

Terrance's goal for this meeting was clear: to discuss ways for him and Calvary's members to engage more with those outside of their walls. He had already started spending his mornings at the local coffee shop, working on his sermon and getting to know the community.

"You know," Terrance says, carefully selecting his words, "this pie reminds me of what we're aiming for at Calvary. We're taking the treasures of our traditions, the recipes that have fed us for generations, and discovering new ways to share them with a hungry world." He watches as understanding dawns on Carolyn and Jonathan's faces. Terrance felt a bridge was formed over a slice of pie, linking the past they cherish and the future they are building together.

Building Bridges: Forming the Core Team

The lively coffee shop buzzes with energy as Terrance happily settles into a seat across from Oliver Williams. The young man's eyes shine with enthusiasm, his hands animatedly expressing his ideas as he shares his exciting vision for Calvary Church's music program. "Pastor, picture this!" Oliver leaned in, his excitement shining through. "We could kick things off with a small praise band, starting with just guitar and drums. Then, little by little, we can weave in more contemporary worship songs. It would feel like a beautiful spiritual resurrection through music!"

Terrance nodded, excited. "I love your enthusiasm, Oliver. How do you think this will attract younger members?"

Oliver's eyes lit up even more as he leaned forward, his voice brimming with passion. "Pastor, music is a powerful way to connect with people, especially the younger generation. They crave authenticity, engagement, community, and relevance in worship. By starting with a small praise band and gradually introducing more songs that speak to the void in their lives, we can create worship experiences that feel uplifting and deeply spiritual."

Terrance listened intently, appreciating Oliver's insights. "That makes sense. It's about meeting them where they are, right?"

"Exactly!" Oliver exclaims. "We can also use social media to share snippets of our worship sessions, invite local musicians to join us, and even host open mic nights. This way, we're not just a church inside the four walls but a vibrant part of the community."

Terrance smiles, envisioning the possibilities. "I can see it now—a place where everyone feels welcome and inspired. Let's make it happen, Oliver."

Oliver's grin broadens. "That's what makes it beautiful! Modern music resonates with young people in a way that traditional hymns sometimes don't. It's relatable, it's—"

"Excuse me, might I share a little thought?" A warm voice interjects. Terrance glances up and spots Jimmy Rodriguez, the beloved retired music teacher, standing next to their table. With a smile, he cradles a steaming mug of coffee in his weathered hands.

Terrance nodded, appreciating Jimmy's wisdom. "That's an excellent point, Jimmy. Oliver, what Mr. Rodriguez is saying is that while we innovate, we shouldn't forget the foundation that has brought us here."

Oliver's eyes brighten as he considers this: Should we mix traditional hymns with contemporary worship songs?

Jimmy nods, his smile widening. "Exactly. Imagine a service where we start with a beloved hymn everyone knows, then transition into a modern worship song. It creates a bridge between generations, allowing everyone to feel connected."

Terrance adds, "It's about honoring our past while embracing the future. This way, we can attract younger members without losing the essence of what makes Calvary special."

Oliver's enthusiasm returned in full force. "I love it! We can create a worship experience that's rich and diverse, appealing to all ages!"

Jimmy pats Oliver on the back. "That's the spirit, my boy. Music unites us all."

Terrance is filled with excitement and hope as he looks at the two men. "Let's work together to make this vision a reality."

Terrance relaxes a bit, his thoughts buzzing with excitement. This is just the kind of conversation we've been hoping for, he thinks to himself. Then, with a warm smile, he asks, "Jimmy, what ideas do you have for updating our music program while still keeping our cherished traditions alive?"

Jimmy's fingers tap a gentle rhythm on the table. "Maybe we begin by arranging some beloved hymns with a contemporary twist. Then, as our congregation feels more comfortable, we can introduce new songs that align with our theological foundations."

Terrance observes as Oliver's expression changes from skepticism to intrigue. "That . . . that could work," Oliver states slowly. "We could even involve some of the older members in the process and get their input."

Terrance exits the coffee shop, feeling clarity and motivation. Over the next week, he spends time in prayer, seeking guidance on who should be part of the core team based on Merle's wise counsel. As he reflects on the qualities needed, he carefully considers each potential member.

He finally felt at peace and had a clear path forward. He decides on Oliver, whose enthusiasm for music and strong communication skills will be vital. With his empathy and understanding, Jimmy will help bridge the gap between tradition and innovation. Merle, of course, with his resilience and faith, will lead the team with unwavering commitment.

Carolyn's deep commitment to the church's mission and values will ensure they stay true to their purpose. Jonathan's open-mindedness and creativity will help them embrace new ideas while respecting traditions.

And Sarah Chen, with her diverse perspective and problem-solving abilities, will bring fresh insights and practical solutions to the challenges they face.

With this diverse and dedicated team, Terrance feels confident that they can navigate the challenges ahead and create a worship experience that honors Calvary's rich traditions while embracing new opportunities for growth and connection. He feels a surge of hope, realizing that this is the harmony they've been seeking—a blend of tradition and innovation, guided by faith and mutual respect.

After a week of prayer and reflection, Terrance felt confident about his core team selection. He reached out to each member individually, sharing his vision and inviting them to join him on this important mission. Oliver, Jimmy, Merle, Carolyn, Jonathan, and Sarah Chen accepted eagerly, ready to contribute their unique strengths to the church's future.

With the team assembled, Terrance knows it's time to take the next step. He schedules a meeting in the church basement, which holds history and potential. As the day approaches, he feels a mix of nerves and excitement, knowing that this gathering begins a transformative journey for Calvary Church.

The church basement hums with nervous energy as Terrance descends creaky wooden stairs. His heart quickens, sensing the weight of the moment. This is it, he thinks, the first step toward real change. He enters the room, greeted by the eager faces of his core team. He is ready to blend tradition and innovation, guided by faith and mutual respect.

As the core team members start to gather, the church basement fills with anticipation. Oliver, Jimmy, Merle, Carolyn, Jonathan, and Sarah Chen each take their seats, exchanging warm greetings and excited smiles. The room hums with nervous energy, a blend of hope and determination.

Once everyone is settled, Pastor Terrance stands at the head of the table. He takes a deep breath and, with a calm and steady voice, says, "Let's open this meeting with a prayer."

The team bows their heads as Terrance prays, "Heavenly Father, we thank You for bringing us together today. We ask for Your guidance and wisdom as we embark on this journey to revitalize Calvary's mission. May You open new doors with new opportunities for growth. Help us work together in harmony, respecting each other's perspectives and staying true to our mission. May Your presence be with us, and may Your will be done in all that we do. Amen."

As Terrance finishes the prayer, a sense of peace and unity fills the room. The team is ready to take the first steps toward real change.

"As we move forward," Terrance explains, "it's paramount that each of us understands our specific roles and how we can contribute to this vision."

He turns to Carolyn, who has always been a pillar of support. "Carolyn, your deep commitment to our mission and values will be crucial. You'll lead our youth outreach programs, ensuring we stay true to our purpose while engaging with the community."

Next, he addresses Jimmy, who is known for his innovative ideas. You possess the tools that will help us embrace these new concepts. You will oversee the integration of contemporary worship styles, blending them seamlessly with our traditions. Flexibility and creativity

Terrance then looks at Oliver, whose enthusiasm for music is infectious. "Oliver, your role will be to lead our music program. Your strong communication skills will be key in coordinating with musicians and ensuring our worship is both engaging and spiritually enriching."

He turned to Jonathan, whose wisdom and experience were invaluable. "Jonathan, your empathy and understanding will guide us in making thoughtful decisions. You'll be our liaison with the congregation, addressing their concerns and helping them embrace the changes."

Finally, he addresses Merle, whose resilience and faith have always inspired him. "Merle, your leadership and initiative will drive our projects forward. You'll be responsible for problem-solving and ensuring we stay focused on our goals."

As the conversation flows, Terrance realizes this is the harmony they've been seeking—a blend of tradition and innovation, guided by faith. With this diverse and dedicated team, he feels confident they can navigate the challenges ahead and create a worship experience that honors Calvary's traditions while embracing new opportunities for growth and connection.

The room, typically reserved for potlucks and Sunday school, now feels like sacred ground. Folding chairs create a tight circle, each seat occupied by a familiar or new face. Terrance's gaze sweeps across his core team: Oliver, practically buzzing with excitement; Carolyn, her hands clasped tightly in her lap; and a few others, their expressions a mix of anticipation and apprehension.

"Thank you all so much for being here," Terrance starts, his voice calm despite the nervousness he feels inside. "We're gathered here today because we all share a deep love for Calvary Church and want to see it flourish." He takes his seat, keenly aware of the expectations weighing down on him. "Lord, guide our path," he prays silently.

Oliver leans forward, unable to hold back any longer. "Pastor, may I?" At Terrance's nod, he bursts into an impassioned speech. "We need to act now. Contemporary worship, digital outreach, and community events that resonate with young people—these aren't just ideas; they're necessities!"

Terrance observes the others, watching Oliver's remarks elicit sparks of enthusiasm in some individuals while causing frowns of concern in others. He is akin to a blazing comet, Terrance contemplates, radiant yet potentially destructive if not guided carefully.

"Just think about it," Oliver continues, his hands gesturing enthusiastically. "A lively praise band, screens displaying lyrics, maybe even—"

"Screens?" Carolyn interjects, her delicate voice subtly interrupting Oliver's enthusiasm. "Oliver, dear, our stained-glass windows have told God's grace story for generations. Do we really need screens?"

Terrance senses the room's energy shift, teetering on a precarious edge. "How do I bridge this gap and keep this fragile coalition moving forward?" he wonders, searching for words that will unite rather than divide. Terrance takes a deep breath, his fingers instinctively tracing the worn edges of his Bible. "Friends, let me share a story with you. Terrance pauses, glancing around the room and making eye contact with everyone. "In Genesis 41, Joseph interprets Pharaoh's dream about seven years of abundance followed by seven years of famine. Joseph didn't just interpret; he prepared. He stored grain during the good years to sustain Egypt through the hard times. This wasn't about rejecting the past or blindly embracing the future. It was about wisdom, foresight, and balance."

Terrance leans forward, his dark eyes shining with purpose. "We're at a crossroads, much like Egypt. We must prepare for our future while honoring our past. It's not about screens versus stained glass; it's about finding a way to let God's light and the message of the Gospel shine through both."

He notices Sarah Chen sitting quietly in the corner, her fingers absently sketching in her ever-present notebook. "Sarah," he says gently, "you've been quiet. As someone who has restored historic churches, what are your thoughts?"

Sarah looks up, her eyes thoughtful. "Joseph's story is a perfect analogy for what we're facing. Just as he preserved the grain to sustain Egypt, we must preserve the things that can never be compromised, the Truth of God's Word, and our core beliefs. These things sustain our faith community. But we must also be open to new ways of sharing God's message. Restoration isn't just about maintaining the old; it's about integrating the old with the new to create something even more beautiful."

Terrance nods, feeling a surge of hope. "Exactly. We can honor our past while preparing for the future, ensuring that Calvary remains a beacon of faith and community. Let's work together to find that balance, just as Joseph did."

The team feels inspired and guided by faith and mutual respect. With this renewed sense of purpose, they are prepared to navigate the challenges ahead and create a new community that honors Calvary's legacy.

Sarah Chen has a rich background in architecture and design, specializing in the restoration and modernization of historic buildings. Her career began with a passion for preserving the beauty and integrity of old structures while making them functional for contemporary use. She has worked on numerous projects, transforming outdated spaces into vibrant, modern environments without losing their original charm.

Sarah's approach is both creative and practical. She believes in maintaining the essence of a building—its unique character and historical significance—while integrating modern amenities and technologies. Her projects often involve updating plumbing, electrical systems, and accessibility features, ensuring that the spaces are not only beautiful but also efficient and welcoming.

Her expertise lies in striking a balance between old and new, blending traditional architectural elements with innovative design solutions. Sarah's work is characterized by thoughtful planning, attention to detail, and a deep respect for the history of the spaces she transforms. Her ability to envision and execute these changes has earned her a reputation as a skilled and sensitive designer, capable of breathing new life into cherished structures. Her insights are invaluable as they navigate the challenges of blending tradition with innovation.

Terrance watches, captivated, as a rough blueprint emerges in Sarah's expert hands. "Maybe we could install retractable screens," she proposes, "that remain hidden when not in use, maintaining the traditional aesthetic. This would allow us to create a flexible space for traditional and contemporary worship styles." As Sarah elaborates on her vision, Terrance accepts this as the crucial element they have been searching for. He reflects on how this innovation can enhance worship and expand on Carolyn and Jonathan's ideas.

Building Bridges: Forming the Core Team

Sarah's words fill the room with almost tangible energy as they resonate. Terrance observes his team, encouraged by how well this first meeting progresses. Oliver, typically restless, leaned forward in his chair, nodding enthusiastically. Even Carolyn, her initial skepticism faded, seemed thoughtful and engaged.

Terrance turned to Carolyn and Jonathan. "Carolyn, your family's outreach programs can now include community events that utilize this flexible space. Imagine hosting traditional hymn sing-alongs and contemporary worship nights, inviting everyone to celebrate the richness of our worship styles."

Jonathan adds, "We can also use the screens for multimedia presentations during sermons, making them more engaging and relevant to younger members. This blend of old and new is sure to resonate with our diverse congregation."

Jimmy, inspired by the discussion, spoke up next. "To improve children's programming and community outreach, we can use this space for interactive Bible lessons and community workshops. The retractable screens can display educational content and activities, making learning fun and engaging for kids."

Terrance feels empowered, and each member contributes their unique ideas to create a vibrant and inclusive worship experience. "This is the harmony we've been seeking—a blend of culture and innovation. Let's work together to make this vision a reality. We've got work ahead of us, but together, with faith as our foundation, we can create something truly remarkable."

As the meeting draws to a close, Terrance assigns specific tasks to each core team member. This ensures that their unique strengths and expertise are utilized effectively.

Carolyn and Jonathan exchanged determined looks as they were responsible for developing outreach programs for children that engage the community. They will focus on creating activities and events that connect with local families and foster a sense of belonging.

Jimmy, with his calm demeanor and deep understanding of worship, nods as he accepts his task. He will integrate contemporary worship styles into the services, seeking ways to blend modern worship songs with traditional hymns to create a worship experience that resonates with all generations.

Guided by Grace

Oliver, always brimming with enthusiasm, eagerly takes on the role of leading the music program. He will coordinate with musicians, plan worship sets, and ensure that the music enhances the spiritual atmosphere of the services. He also plans to explore opportunities to involve local musicians and host musical events.

Terrance has committed to finding effective community outreach programs in the area. He aims to identify initiatives Calvary Church can adopt and implement to strengthen its connection with the local community.

Merle, with his steady leadership and unwavering faith, will drive leadership and initiative within the team and the congregation. He will focus on fostering leadership skills, encouraging members to take on projects, and ensuring that the team stays motivated and on track.

Sarah, with her creative vision and practical expertise, will oversee the modernization of the worship and meeting space. She envisions integrating retractable screens and other modern amenities that enhance functionality while preserving the church's traditional aesthetic.

As Terrance watches his team, "We've got work ahead of us," he says, his voice filled with conviction, "but together, with faith as our foundation, we can create something truly remarkable."

As the core team exits the building, their spirits high from the productive meeting, Terrance feels a sense of accomplishment. They chat animatedly about their plans, each member eager to begin their assigned tasks. However, as they step outside, Terrance's attention is drawn to Jack Whitmore and Henry Jenkins, huddled nearby. Their hushed voices exude an air of conspiracy that sends a chill down Terrance's spine.

"Is everything alright, Pastor?" Oliver asks, noticing Terrance's distraction.

Terrance forces a smile, trying to shake off the unease. "Yes, Oliver. Let's stay focused on our goals. We've got a lot of work ahead of us."

Terrance can't help but feel a lingering sense of concern as the team disperses. He knows that navigating change will require vision, dedication, and resilience in the face of opposition. With faith as their foundation, he hopes they can overcome challenges and create a worship experience that honors Calvary's rich traditions while embracing new opportunities for growth and connection.

"Pastor?" Carolyn's voice cuts through his reverie. "Are you sure everything's alright?" Terrance turns to her, mustering a warm smile. "Just considering the journey ahead, Carolyn. It's quite the mountain we have to climb, isn't it?"

Carolyn nods, her eyes reflecting both concern and determination. "But we're not climbing this journey alone, right? God is with us at every step, guiding us along the way." Her words resonate deeply with Terrance.

"You're right," he agrees, feeling a renewed sense of purpose. "And we have each other, too. That's what makes this church family so special."

As Terrance heads home, feeling a mix of exhaustion and exhilaration. He opens the front door and steps inside, greeted by the comforting warmth of his home. Beth, his wife, leaves Grant's room after putting their son to bed. She looks up, her eyes filled with curiosity and eagerness to hear about the critical meeting.

"Hey, love," Beth says, walking over to Terrance. "How did it go?"

Terrance smiles, feeling a surge of gratitude for her support. "It went really well. We had some great discussions and set some important goals."

Beth leads him to the living room, where they settle onto the couch. "Tell me everything," she says, her tone encouraging.

Terrance begins recounting the meeting, describing how each team member was assigned specific tasks: "Carolyn and Jonathan will develop outreach programs for children that engage the community. Jimmy will integrate contemporary worship styles into our services. Oliver is leading the music program, and I will search for effective community outreach programs in the area. Merle will drive leadership and initiative, and Sarah will oversee the modernization of our worship and meeting space."

Beth listens intently, nodding along. "It sounds like you have a strong team. How do you feel about the direction you're heading?"

Terrance leans back, reflecting on the day's events. "I feel hopeful. Everyone brought unique ideas to the table, and there was a real sense of purpose and unity. We aim to blend tradition and innovation, guided by faith and mutual respect."

Beth smiles, her eyes shining with pride. "That's wonderful, Terrance. It sounds like you're on the right path. I'm sure the congregation will respond positively to these changes."

Terrance takes her hand, feeling a deep sense of connection. "Thank you for always being here for me. I believe we can create something truly remarkable with your support and the team's dedication."

As they sat together, processing the meeting's outcome, Terrance knew the journey ahead may be challenging, but with faith as their foundation, he knew they could navigate the changes and build a vibrant, inclusive worship experience for Calvary Church.

Addressing Concerns About Rapid Change

1. **Gradual Implementation:** Many churches implement changes gradually to give members time to adjust. This can involve beginning with small modifications and progressively integrating more significant changes.

2. **Open Communication:** Transparent communication is crucial. Church leaders should clarify the reasons for changes, how these align with the church's mission, and the benefits they will bring. Regular updates and open forums for discussion can help address concerns and build trust.

3. **Involvement and Ownership:** Engaging congregation members in the decision-making process can minimize resistance. Creating committees or focus groups that encompass diverse perspectives ensures that changes align with the community's needs and desires.

4. **Education and Training:** Educating and training members about new initiatives can help them understand and embrace changes. Workshops, informational sessions, and resources can provide the knowledge and skills necessary for adaptation.

5. **Respect for Tradition:** Balancing innovation with respect for tradition is essential. Churches can preserve core elements of their worship and community activities while integrating new practices. This approach honors the past while embracing the future.

6. **Feedback and Adaptation:** Regularly seeking feedback from the congregation and being willing to make adjustments based on their input demonstrates that their opinions are valued. This can help reassure members that changes are being made thoughtfully and inclusively.

By implementing these strategies, church leaders can address concerns regarding rapid changes and promote necessary transformation in a manner that reassures and engages their congregation.

Building Bridges: Forming the Core Team

Discussion Questions

Balancing Tradition and Change:

1. How can leaders balance the need for change with the importance of preserving traditions? What role do personal gestures, such as Carolyn's apple pie, play in bridging the past and future?

Seeking Insights and Collaboration

2. How can leaders effectively engage enthusiastic members such as Oliver Williams to drive innovation while ensuring alignment with the church's values?

3. How can leaders integrate insights from seasoned members like Jimmy Rodriguez to balance tradition with innovation?

Strategy Sessions and Team Dynamics

4. What are some effective ways to encourage open dialogue and collaboration among team members with differing views during strategy sessions?

5. How can leaders mediate conflicts between advocates of radical change and those who prefer a more measured approach? What biblical stories or principles can guide these discussions?

Vision and Compromise

6. How can leaders develop a cohesive vision that bridges tradition and innovation, as suggested by Sarah Chen? What steps can be taken to ensure this vision aligns with God's purpose?

7. How can leaders promote a sense of unity and renewed purpose among team members during periods of transformation?

Observing Opposition and Seeking Guidance

8. How should leaders manage skepticism from congregation members such as Eleanor Davis? What strategies can be implemented to address their concerns and gain their support?

9. How important is it for leaders to seek guidance and support from trusted advisors and mentors? How can these relationships be developed and sustained?

Personal Reflection and Perseverance

10. How might leaders utilize moments of personal reflection and prayer to sustain their resolve and navigate the challenges that lie ahead?

5

Forging the Path Forward

"Commit to the Lord whatever you do, and he will establish your plans."
—Proverbs 16:3

Defining Your Trophy

> What is your trophy? Most organizations have no idea what they are trying to accomplish or, worse yet, why they exist. An organization's vision determines its direction. Vision is the ability to visualize the desired future in a compelling way. Vision is more powerful when developed as a team and inspires action. To be relevant, a vision must be right for the times, the organization, and the people. Shared vision promotes faith rather than fear. That shared vision motivates people to act and commit to an idea and agenda greater than themselves. Any worthwhile vision requires risk-taking. If that vision is godly, it glorifies God, not people. Godly visions describe where the congregation believes God wants the church to be in the future. Rather than thinking about vision as a calendar, think about it as a compass.

The church library, a sanctuary of wisdom and quiet reflection, was bathed in the afternoon sun's soft glow. Dust particles danced in the beams of light that filtered through the stained glass windows. They cast colorful patterns on the old wooden tables and shelves lined with ancient tomes.

The core team gathered in this hallowed space after completing their assigned tasks. Their faces were a mix of excitement and focus.

Pastor Terrance, the team's guiding force, stood at the head of the table, his eyes twinkling with pride. "We've come a long way," he began, his voice resonating with the weight of their collective efforts. Today, we share our findings and lay the foundation for our ministry plan."

Merle, tasked with leadership development, spread out his notes, detailing strategies to empower and nurture future leaders within the congregation. His voice was steady, and each word was carefully chosen to convey his research depth. "Our community is diverse, with unique challenges and opportunities. We must tailor our approach to developing effective leaders."

Carolyn and Jonathan, who had been exploring children's programs, presented their vision for engaging and nurturing the church's youngest members. Their enthusiasm was infectious, and the room pulsed with energy as they spoke. "We need to create a safe, fun, and educational environment for our children, fostering their spiritual growth and sense of belonging."

Jimmy, who merges classic hymns with a modern twist, shared his innovative approach to worship music. His passion for blending tradition with contemporary elements brought excitement. "Our music should resonate with all generations, bridging the gap between the old and the new."

Oliver, who developed the music ministry, outlined his plans for a vibrant and intergenerational musical community. His vision was clear, and his words inspired hope: "We will build a ministry that celebrates diversity and encourages participation from all members, creating a harmonious and uplifting worship experience."

Sarah Chen was redesigning the church's sacred space and meeting area and revealed her plans for a welcoming and serene environment. Her gentle demeanor and empathetic words brought calm and purpose. "Our space must reflect our values and provide a sanctuary for reflection, connection, and growth."

As each member contributed their findings, the room was filled with unity and shared purpose. Ideas flowed freely, and the beginnings of a ministry plan took shape, rooted in the team's collective wisdom and dedication.

And so, in the quiet embrace of the church library, the core team birthed a new ministry. This is a testament to their unwavering faith and commitment to serving their community. With all the findings in hand, Pastor Terrance looked around the table, his heart swelling with gratitude.

"Thank you all for your hard work and dedication. We've laid a strong foundation today. Let's continue to build on this and create something truly impactful for our community."

The team nodded in agreement, their spirits lifted by the shared sense of purpose. As they left the church library, they carried with them the beginnings of a ministry plan, ready to transform their vision into reality.

Terrance and Merle received an email invitation to attend a mission conference at a large neighboring church. The event promised to bring together key leaders and innovative thinkers in ministry. Recognizing the opportunity to learn and grow, they decided to attend together, eager to share the best practices they would learn from fellow brothers in ministry.

The following week, Terrance found himself in a bustling conference room in a nearby town. The air was charged with the exchange of ideas and the hum of enthusiastic conversations. He glanced around, taking in the diverse array of attendees, each representing different facets of community engagement.

Turning to Merle, who stood beside him with a notebook in hand, Terrance, his mind open to inhale new knowledge and concepts, "I never realized there were so many different approaches to community engagement," he admitted, his voice tinged with awe.

Merle nodded, his eyes scanning the room. "It's incredible, isn't it? There's so much we can learn here. Let's make the most of it and bring back some valuable insights for our ministry."

Pastor Terrance was particularly interested in strategies to revitalize an existing congregation, eager to breathe new life into his church community. Conversely, Merle focused on developing leaders and was keen to empower and nurture future leaders within the congregation. Merle says,. "The body of Christ has many parts, Terrance. Each community must discover its own way to serve."

As they listen to a passionate speaker discuss innovative outreach programs, Terrance notices how easily Merle engages with other participants during the break. The older man's gentle authority and wealth of experience seem to naturally draw people to him. "You've really got a knack for connecting with people, Merle," Terrance observes with admiration.

Merle chuckles softly. "Years in the business world taught me that the most important skill is listening. Everyone has a story to tell, and often, that's where the best ideas come from."

Terrance absorbs this wisdom, his mind already racing with how to apply it back home. "I want to learn from everyone here," he says earnestly. "There's so much potential for growth if we're willing to open our minds and hearts."

As the workshop progresses, Terrance furiously enters the data on his computer. His enthusiasm for revitalizing Calvary Church deepens with every new idea presented. Now that the ministry conference has ended, Terrance and Merle are brimming with excitement to share the thriving ministry examples they have discovered. Inspired by the innovative approaches and successful strategies they encountered, they are eager to bring these insights back to their core team.

Later that evening, the fluorescent lights in Calvary Church's fellowship hall hummed softly as Terrance stood before a large whiteboard with a marker. Carolyn, Oliver, and Merle were seated around a table covered with notes and open laptops. "Alright, team!" Terrance said, his warm brown eyes sparkling with enthusiasm. "We've gathered some incredible ideas from the conference, and I'm excited to see how we can integrate them into our ministry plan."

Merle nodded in agreement, ready to share his notes on leadership development. Carolyn and Oliver leaned forward, their curiosity piqued by the promise of new strategies and fresh perspectives. The room buzzed with anticipation as the team prepared to embark on the next phase of their journey, armed with newfound knowledge and a shared vision for the future.

Terrance began by sharing a specific example from a local congregation that faced challenges similar to Calvary's. "This church was struggling financially, and their attendance was dwindling," he explained. "But they experienced a remarkable revitalization through a ministry aimed at young mothers. A group of men who loved working on cars partnered to offer single moms free oil changes at first, then minor car repairs. This outreach transformed the culture of the congregation, and young families started to show up on Sunday mornings."

The team listened intently, inspired by the success story. Carolyn's eyes lit up with ideas for similar outreach programs, while Oliver considered how the music ministry could support such initiatives. Merle jotted down notes, thinking about how leadership development could help sustain these efforts.

"Let's brainstorm how we can adapt this approach to fit our community's needs," Terrance suggested, his voice filled with hope. "We have the potential to make a real difference here."

With renewed determination, the team dove into their discussion, ready to turn inspiration into action and breathe new life into Calvary Church.

Terrance continued, sharing another example that had caught his attention. "One church found success by hosting community playdates. These events provided children a safe and fun environment while allowing parents to connect and build relationships. This initiative helped the church become a hub for young families."

Carolyn's face lit up. "That's brilliant! We could organize similar events and create a welcoming space for families in our community."

Merle added, "Another congregation emphasized partnering with parents to support their role as primary faith influencers. They created programs that equipped and encouraged parents, fostering a home-centered, church-supported culture."

Oliver nodded thoughtfully. "We could integrate that into our children's programs, ensuring parents feel supported and involved."

Terrance then shared a story about a church that revitalized its community by focusing on small groups. "These groups provided a space for meaningful conversations about faith, helping members build deeper connections with each other and with God."

Merle smiled. "Small groups are essential for building a strong, supportive community. We should definitely prioritize this."

Terrance also mentioned a church that implemented practices to nurture the longevity of their ministry leaders. "By supporting both paid staff and volunteers, they ensured that leaders could thrive in their roles and make a lasting impact."

Merle jotted down notes. "Leadership development is crucial. We need to create a sustainable model for our leaders."

Carolyn leans forward, her glasses shining in the light. "We should also think about something for our older members. Maybe a weekly social gathering with hymn singing and light refreshments?" "What a fantastic idea, Carolyn!" Terrance smiles as he adds it to the ever-growing list. "We really want to be sure that everyone, no matter their age, feels included!"

Carolyn nods with a thoughtful smile. "That sounds very wise, Terrance! Change is essential, but we should ensure we get buy-in from other key stakeholders. Everyone's voice deserves to be heard throughout the process. Maybe we could hold listening meetings in a town hall format to gather their input and create an atmosphere of open communication."

Finally, Terrance shared an example of a congregation that improved their outreach efforts through effective communication. "They utilized social media, newsletters, and regular updates to keep members informed and engaged."

Oliver's eyes sparkled with ideas. "We can enhance our communication strategies to better connect with our congregation and the wider community."

As the core team prepared to disperse, Terrance outlined the next steps for each member, ensuring everyone had a clear direction moving forward.

Carolyn: "You'll lead the initiative to organize community playdates. Start by planning the first event, identifying suitable locations, and reaching out to families in our community. Let's create a welcoming space for children and parents to connect."

Oliver: "You'll integrate the parent partnership programs into our children's ministry. Develop workshops and resources that equip and encourage parents as primary faith influencers. Collaborate with Carolyn to ensure these programs complement the playdates."

Merle: "You'll focus on developing our small groups. Create a sustainable model that fosters rich relational and meaningful conversations about faith. Begin by identifying potential leaders, and we will provide them with the necessary training and support."

Jimmy: "You'll continue merging classic hymns with a modern twist for our worship services. Work closely with Oliver to incorporate these musical elements into the broader music ministry, ensuring our worship resonates with all generations."

Sarah Chen: "You'll finalize redesigning our church's sacred space and meeting area. Ensure the new design reflects our values and provides a welcoming environment for reflection, connection, and growth. Coordinate with the team to integrate these changes smoothly. Once these plans are done, we will have to present them to our trustees and the whole church."

Terrance: "I'll oversee the overall implementation of our mission plans and enhance our communication strategies. I'll work on utilizing social media, newsletters, and regular updates to keep our congregation informed and engaged. Let's make sure everyone feels connected and involved."

With their next steps clearly defined, the team left the fellowship hall with a clear plan and a shared commitment to transforming their vision into reality, ready to breathe new life into Calvary Church.

After the meeting, Terrance and Merle lingered in the fellowship hall, reflecting on the day's discussions. Terrance felt a wave of self-doubt wash over him. "Merle, I'm feeling a bit overwhelmed. Do I have what it takes to lead Calvary through these mission plans?"

Merle's presence was a comforting anchor. He placed a reassuring hand on Terrance's shoulder. "Remember, Terrance, 'For I know the plans I have for you,' declares the Lord, 'plans to prosper you and not to harm you, plans to give you hope and a bright future.'"

Terrance managed a soft smile.

We have some fantastic ideas and can make a meaningful difference together.

Merle nodded, his eyes filled with encouragement. "You're not alone in this. We have a strong team, and we'll navigate these challenges and bring our vision to life. That's what I'm here for, son. Remember, 'As iron sharpens iron, so one person sharpens another.' We're in this together."

Over the following days, they worked diligently, organizing community playdates, developing parent partnership programs, fostering small groups, and enhancing communication strategies. Their collective efforts culminated in a town hall meeting, where they would present their ideas to the members of Calvary Church.

The fellowship hall buzzed with anticipation as the congregation gathered, eager to hear the plans that promised to breathe new life into their beloved church. The core team stood at the front, ready to share their vision and hoping to receive positive feedback from the members.

However, not everyone was excited about the new ideas. Eleanor, Henry, and Jack Whitmore, who had just returned from his winter home in Arizona, expressed their reservations. Eleanor's brow furrowed as she listened, Henry crossed his arms skeptically, and Jack shook his head, clearly unconvinced.

Sensing the tension, Terrance took a deep breath and addressed the concerns with empathy and openness. "We understand that change can be challenging," he began, his voice calm and reassuring. "Our goal is to honor our traditions while also embracing new opportunities to grow and serve our community. We value your feedback and want to ensure that everyone feels heard and included in this process."

Eleanor spoke up first, her voice tinged with worry. "I'm concerned about the pace of change. It feels like everything is happening so quickly. How can we ensure we're not losing sight of what's important?"

Terrance nodded, acknowledging her concern. "Eleanor, your point is valid. We will take a measured approach, ensuring that each step is carefully considered and that we maintain our core values throughout this process."

Henry then voiced his concern. "How are we going to fund these changes? We already have financial challenges, and I'm worried about the additional strain on our resources."

Merle stepped forward to address Henry's concern. "Henry, funding is a critical aspect, and we have plans to approach this responsibly. We'll explore grants, fundraising events, and partnerships with local businesses to support our initiatives. Transparency and careful budgeting will be key."

Finally, Jack Whitmore, in a voice heavy with emotion, shared his thoughts: "I don't recognize the church my wife and I joined years ago. She recently passed away, and I'm struggling to see how these changes fit with the church we loved."

Terrance's heart went out to Jack. "Jack, I'm deeply sorry for your loss. Terrance felt inspired to expand on Calvary's rich traditions. "Calvary Church has always been a place of traditional worship, where hymns and liturgy create a sense of reverence and consistency. Our close-knit congregation is like a family, supporting each other through life's ups and downs. We have a long history in this community, and our roots run deep."

He continued, his voice filled with hope. "We've found wonderful ways to celebrate our traditions while warmly inviting those who may feel disconnected from faith to join us. For example, our community playdates will provide children a safe and fun environment, allowing parents to connect and build relationships. This initiative will help us become a hub for young families, just as we have always been a cornerstone of this community."

Terrance looked around the room, seeing the mix of emotions on the congregation's faces. "Our parent partnership programs will equip and encourage parents, fostering a home-centered, church-supported culture. Small groups will provide a space for meaningful conversations about faith, helping members build deeper connections with each other and with God."

Merle added, "We'll also implement practices to nurture the longevity of our ministry leaders, ensuring they can thrive in their roles and make a lasting impact. Effective communication will keep everyone informed and engaged, strengthening our sense of community."

The room fell silent as the congregation considered the words of their leaders. The core team hoped that they could address the concerns through open dialogue and collaboration and build a stronger, more united church community.

Mrs. Pearson, one of Eleanor's closest friends, leans forward. "That sounds promising, Pastor, but how can we make sure we don't lose our identity in the process?"

Terrance's mind races as he recalls Merle's advice on adaptability. "That's an excellent question, Mrs. Pearson. Our goal isn't to erase who we are, but to expand on our strong foundation. Think of it as adding new branches to a healthy tree."

Eleanor pressed in, "Could I ask how you plan to make this happen, pastor?"

Terrance paused, "We could start small. Perhaps we could begin with a monthly community dinner, inviting both members and non-members to break bread together. It's a chance to share our fellowship while opening our doors wider." As he speaks, Terrance notices a change in the atmosphere. The initial tension starts to fade, giving way to cautious curiosity. He silently thanks God for the guidance that brought him to this moment.

"I must admit," Eleanor says slowly, her voice softer than usual, "the idea has merit. But what about our Sunday services? We can't just abandon our hymns and liturgy."

Terrance nods with empathy. "Absolutely not, Mrs. Davis. Our traditional service is the heart of our church. What if we introduced an additional, more contemporary service while keeping our main service unchanged? It could attract new faces without disrupting what we hold dear." As the discussion continues, Terrance feels an increasing sense of hope. He's walking a tightrope, balancing tradition and progress, but with each carefully chosen word, he sees the possibility of unity emerging.

As the meeting comes to a close, Terrance's eyes scan the room, noting the glaring absence of two key figures. Jack and Henry's vacant chairs speak volumes and a knot forms in his stomach. He takes a deep breath, reminding himself of the importance of patience and perseverance. "Thank you all for your time and open-mindedness," Terrance says, his warm brown eyes connecting with each person's gaze. "I understand that change can be daunting, but I believe we're on the right path."

Eleanor rises, smoothing her tailored skirt. "Well, Pastor," she begins, her tone measured but not unkind. You've certainly given us a lot to consider. I can't say I'm entirely convinced, but . . ." She pauses, her stern expression softening slightly. "I'm willing to pray about it and discuss it further."

Terrance's heart leaps at her words. "That's all I can ask, Mrs. Davis. Thank you."

As the group disperses, Terrance catches Carolyn's eye. She gives him an encouraging nod."

Later, in the sanctuary, Terrance meets with his allies. The late afternoon sun streams through the stained glass windows, enveloping them in a warm, multi-colored glow. "Well, folks," Terrance says, running a hand through his short, dark hair, "I'd say that went better than I expected."

Oliver grins as his untamed hair falls over his forehead. "I think it calls for a celebration. How about we sing a lively rendition of 'Amazing Grace'? With a bit of jazz flair, of course."

Carolyn chuckles softly, her kind features crinkling with amusement. "Oh, Oliver. Always a musician." She turns to Terrance and says, "Before we get carried away with Oliver's jazzed-up hymns, how about we offer a prayer of thanks?"

Terrance nods, appreciative of Carolyn's stabilizing presence. "That's great, Carolyn. Would you like to take the lead?"

As Carolyn's soothing voice fills the sanctuary with words of gratitude, Terrance closes his eyes. He feels a profound sense of unity with the people who have stood by him, even as his mind races with the challenges ahead. Jack and Henry's absence weighs on him, but he pushes the worry aside, focusing instead on their progress. When the prayer ends, Terrance opens his eyes with a determined smile on his face. "Alright, team. We've made a good start, but there's still work ahead. Let's discuss the next steps."

As the others begin discussing logistics, Terrance feels drawn to the pulpit. He steps up, tracing his fingers along the worn wood, and gazes out at the empty pews. In his mind's eye, he envisions them filled with a vibrant, diverse congregation—young families, elderly couples, teenagers with dyed hair, and everything in between. "Lord," he whispers, his dark eyes shining with unshed tears, "guide us as we strive to build Your kingdom here."

The sanctuary seems to hum with possibility. Terrance envisions Bible study groups buzzing with lively discussion, children's laughter echoing through the halls, and community outreach programs transforming lives. He envisions a church that's a beacon of hope, not just on Sundays but every day of the week.

"Are you doing okay up there, Pastor?" Oliver's voice interrupts Terrance's daydream.

Terrance turns, a smile spreading across his face. "More than fine, Oliver. I'm . . . inspired."

Carolyn approaches, her maternal concern clear. "What do you see, Terrance?"

He gestures broadly, his excitement evident. "I envision us living out Acts 2:42–47: a church dedicated to teaching, to fellowship, and to breaking bread together. A place where miracles happen, where needs are met, and where lives are changed."

Merle nods in approval. "That's a powerful vision, son. How do we achieve it?"

Terrance's brow furrows in thought. "One step at a time, with prayer, perseverance, and a whole lot of love."

As the group disperses, Terrance retreats to his office. He settles behind his desk and pulls out a fresh notebook. His pen flies across the page, and he writes down ideas for the upcoming town hall meetings. "Communication is key," he murmurs to himself. "We need to show them that change doesn't mean losing who we are; it means becoming more of who we're meant to be." He pauses, tapping his pen against his chin. "How can I help them see that? Terrance leans back in his chair, his gaze resting on a framed photo of his wife Beth and their son Grant. He smiles, drawing strength from their image. "This isn't just about Calvary Church," he realizes. "It's about creating a legacy of faith for generations to come." In his notebook, he writes down:

Sample Questions for A Town Hall Meeting

Here are some facilitation questions for you to lead a town hall meeting:

1. How can we honor the history of our church while also welcoming new opportunities for growth?
   - Which traditions hold the most significance for you?
   - How can we maintain these traditions while adjusting to present needs?
   - Are there particular aspects of our history we should emphasize in our future plans?

2. What does a thriving, Christ-centered community mean to you?
   - What characteristics define a Christ-centered community?
   - How can we foster deeper connections among our members?
   - What roles do worship, service, and fellowship play in a thriving community?
3. How can we more effectively meet the needs of our broader community?
   - What are the most pressing needs in our local community?
   - How can we leverage our resources and talents to address these needs?
   - Are there specific outreach programs or partnerships we should consider?
4. How can each of us contribute to this vision of renewal?
   - What unique gifts and talents can you bring to our ministry efforts?
   - How can we encourage greater active participation from our congregation?
   - What steps can we take to ensure that everyone feels included and valued in this process?
   - These questions aim to encourage open dialogue and collaboration, assisting the congregation in collectively shaping your church's future.

Terrance sets down his pen, a quiet excitement bubbling inside him. The road ahead won't be easy, but with God's grace and the support of his allies, he knows they can bridge the gap between tradition and transformation. Terrance bows his head in prayer, prepared to face whatever challenges tomorrow may bring.

Discussion Questions

Balancing Innovation with Tradition

1. How can we balance innovation with tradition in our ministry efforts?

2. What are some innovative ideas that can complement our traditional practices?
3. How can we ensure that our innovations respect and honor our church's history?

Preserving Our Church's Past and Traditions

4. What aspects of our church's past and traditions are most important to preserve?
5. Which traditions do you feel are essential to our identity as a church?
6. How can we incorporate these traditions into our new initiatives?

Engaging the Congregation

7. How can we engage our congregation in the process of innovation and renewal?
8. What strategies can we use to gather input and ideas from our members?
9. How can we encourage active participation and ownership of new initiatives?

Overcoming Challenges

10. What are the key challenges we face in implementing new ideas, and how can we overcome them?
11. What potential obstacles might we encounter, and how can we address them?
12. How can we build a culture of openness and adaptability within our church?

Communicating Our Vision

13. How can we effectively communicate our vision for the future to the congregation?
14. What methods can we use to share our plans and gather feedback?

15. How can we ensure that our communication is clear, transparent, and inclusive?

Leadership Roles

16. What role does each leader play in driving innovation while honoring our traditions?
17. How can each of us leverage our unique strengths and talents in this process?
18. What specific actions can we take to support and lead our congregation through this transition?

Measuring Success

19. How can we measure the success of our new initiatives while staying true to our core values?
20. What metrics or indicators can we use to track progress and impact?
21. How can we ensure that our efforts align with our mission and vision as a church?

6

Facing the Storm

> "For they all were trying to make us afraid, saying, 'Their hands will be weakened in the work, and it will not be done.' Now therefore, O God, strengthen my hands." —NEHEMIAH 6:9

Overcoming Resistance

Given the potential for increased resistance and sabotage, it is crucial to consider and prepare for these challenges proactively. This involves conducting thorough risk assessments to identify possible sources of opposition and sabotage, and implementing robust security measures to mitigate these risks. Developing contingency plans to address unexpected disruptions can also ensure swift and effective responses. Training leadership to recognize and respond to signs of sabotage, and fostering a culture of vigilance and resilience, can further enhance preparedness. By taking these steps, organizations can better safeguard their operations and maintain stability in the face of adversity.

The town hall meeting was held in the heart of Calvary's community center, a spacious room with high ceilings and large windows that let in the afternoon light. Rows of chairs were neatly arranged, facing a modest stage where a podium stood ready for speakers. The atmosphere was charged with anticipation as Calvary members and some inactive former members filed in, their murmurs creating a low hum of conversation.

Flanked by his core team, Terrance stood at the front, their expressions a mix of determination and apprehension. They knew this meeting was crucial. The room gradually filled to capacity, with people standing along the walls and in the back, eager to hear what Terrance had to say.

As Terrance stood at the podium, a mix of emotions swirled within him. The weight of the moment was palpable, and he knew that the success of their initiatives hinged on this meeting. His heart raced with a blend of anxiety and determination. He was acutely aware of the critical eyes watching him, ready to dissect his every word.

Terrance's voice remained steady, but internally, he grappled with the pressure. Each question from the audience felt like a test, challenging his resolve and his vision. He felt the sting of skepticism and the burden of proving himself to a community that had its doubts.

Amidst the tension, Terrance found solace in the presence of his wife, Beth. She sat in the front row, her gaze unwavering and filled with quiet encouragement. Beth's support was a constant source of strength for Terrance. Her subtle nods and reassuring smiles reminded him that he wasn't alone in this endeavor.

Beth's quiet encouragement was a beacon of hope. She believed in him and the core team's vision; her faith was a steadying force. Whenever Terrance felt the weight of the criticisms bearing down on him, he would glance at Beth, drawing comfort from her calm demeanor.

Her presence was a silent affirmation that they were on the right path, giving Terrence the courage to face the challenges head-on and to persevere in the face of adversity. With Beth's unwavering support, Terrance found the strength to push through his doubts and fears. Together, they were a united front, ready to overcome any obstacles that came their way.

When the floor was opened for questions, the atmosphere shifted. Critics and detractors, who had been waiting for this moment, seized the opportunity to voice their concerns. One by one, they stood up, their questions pointed and their tone challenging.

"Terrance, how do you plan to address the financial risks involved?" one member asked, her voice tinged with skepticism.

Another stood up, arms crossed, "What about the impact on our local businesses? Have you considered the long-term consequences?"

Terrance listened intently, absorbing the weight of each concern. He responded thoughtfully, acknowledging their points' validity while presenting counterarguments and reassurances. His core team supported him, providing additional insights and data.

Despite the combative nature of the discussion, Terrance remained composed. He knew that facing these criticisms head-on was essential for gaining the community's trust. As the meeting progressed, the tension in the room began to ease, replaced by a sense of cautious optimism.

"Thank you for your questions," Terrance began, his voice steady. "I understand your concerns, and I want to remind everyone of the sermon we heard this morning about Nehemiah and rebuilding the Jerusalem wall."

The room grew quiet as Terrance continued. "Nehemiah faced immense opposition and criticism when he set out to rebuild the wall. People doubted his vision, questioned his motives, and tried to undermine his efforts. But Nehemiah remained steadfast. He listened to the concerns, addressed them, and continued to work towards his goal."

Terrance paused, letting the story sink in. "Like Nehemiah, we are facing challenges and criticisms. However, we can achieve something great for our community by addressing these concerns head-on and working together. It's not just about the physical walls we build, but the trust and unity we foster."

We have been diligently developing initiatives to strengthen our community and enhance our faith-based programs. I'd like to share these plans with you now as a united community. By embracing these initiatives, we can create a stronger, more vibrant church that meets the needs of all its members and continues to grow in faith and service."

Terrance glanced at his notes and continued, "First, Carolyn will lead the initiative to organize community playdates. These events will create a welcoming space for children and parents to connect and build relationships. Carolyn has already started planning the first event, identifying suitable locations, and reaching out to families in our community."

He then turned to Oliver, "Oliver will integrate parent partnership programs into our children's ministry. He will develop workshops and resources that equip and encourage parents as primary faith influencers. Oliver and Carolyn will collaborate to ensure these programs complement the playdates, creating a cohesive support system for families."

Terrance moved on to Merle's role, "Merle will focus on developing our small groups. He is working on creating a sustainable model that fosters rich relational and meaningful conversations about faith. Merle has begun identifying potential leaders and will provide them with the necessary training and support."

Next, he addressed Jimmy's contributions, "Jimmy will continue merging classic hymns with a modern twist for our worship services. He will work closely with Oliver to incorporate these musical elements into the broader music ministry, ensuring our worship resonates with all generations."

Terrance then spoke about Sarah Chen's project, "Sarah Chen will finalize redesigning our church's sacred space and meeting area. She aims to ensure the new design reflects our values and provides a welcoming environment for reflection, connection, and growth. Sarah will coordinate with the team to integrate these changes smoothly and present the final plans to our trustees and the whole church."

Finally, Terrance outlined his responsibilities: "I will oversee the overall implementation of our mission plans and enhance our communication strategies. I will work on utilizing social media, newsletters, and regular updates to keep our congregation informed and engaged. It's important that everyone feels connected and involved in our church's new direction."

Terrance concluded, "I appreciate your feedback and your willingness to engage in this discussion. Let's move forward together, just as Nehemiah did, with determination and hope. Because of our church constitution, the congregation needs to approve the church's new direction. So, once we are done with our quarterly Voter's meeting, we will call for a vote."

"Friends," Terrance says, leaning in, "Calvary Church stands at a crossroads. We have a choice to make: remain stagnant or embrace a new vision for our future." Oliver nods eagerly, his tousled hair bouncing with each movement. Carolyn's brow slightly furrows behind her glasses, but her eyes stay attentive. Terrance continues, his voice gaining momentum. "I believe God is calling us to be a beacon of hope in Oakridge. To achieve this, we need fresh ideas and innovative approaches to engage our community." Eleanor remains silent at first, but in her silence, he can almost hear Eleanor's objections echo. But he pushes forward, driven by the certainty that this is the right path.

The room goes quiet for a moment, and Terrance holds his breath. Then, one by one, his allies nod in agreement. A wave of relief washes over him, mixed with excitement for the journey ahead. "Alright then," he says, a smile spreading across his face. We must act boldly and with purpose," he says, his voice steady. "Together, we can transform this vision into reality and make a lasting impact. Let us move forward with faith, courage, and determination."

The faces in the crowd reflect a kaleidoscope of emotions—hope, skepticism, determination. Some lean forward, eagerness evident in their expressions, while others, like Eleanor, sit back with their arms crossed, fortresses of resistance. The tension is palpable, a tightrope stretched across the room vibrating with the potential for both progress and division. He tries to capture the room's emotions with this acknowledgment, "I know the road ahead may seem daunting, but together, with faith and unity, we can strengthen Calvary's future."

Terrance surveys the assembled members, looking for signs of encouragement amid the doubt. "Change can be difficult," he continues, "but remember Nehemiah. What seemed like an impossible task was accomplished with God's strength and our dedication." His words linger in the air, a lifeline cast into the sea of mixed opinions.

"However, is this truly necessary?" a skeptical voice interjects. It is Jack; his countenance reflects a calculated challenge. "We have managed effectively in this manner for generations. What is the urgency behind implementing changes?"

Others share his concern, and murmurs of agreement ripple through the crowd. Henry chimes in, his voice resonating with authority: "There's wisdom in tradition, Terrance. We need to be cautious not to lose what's important."

Terrance nods thoughtfully, embracing the resistance with steady strength. "I understand where you're coming from," he replies, addressing the gathered voices with a kind yet firm resolve. "While our heritage is incredibly important, we must evolve and grow to inspire the next generation. Let's shine brightly for everyone, not just for ourselves!" A mix of support and dissent fills the room, voices overlapping in a chaotic chorus. Some shout encouragement while others shake their heads, the division becoming more pronounced with each passing moment. Beth's eyes find Terrance's, a silent testament to her unwavering belief, urging him to press on.

During this moment, Eleanor rises suddenly, her chair producing a harsh sound as it scrapes across the floor. The atmosphere shifts to silence, and all attention is drawn to her as she directs a piercing gaze at Terrance. "We've been down this road before," she asserts, her voice slicing through the stillness with sharp clarity. "I won't see this church torn apart again."

She strides toward the door, her footsteps echoing in the stillness, leaving a trail of shocked whispers in her wake. The tension that had been simmering now boils over, a palpable force that lingers even after the door slams shut.

As Terrance stood at the front, absorbing the reactions of the congregation, a moment of reflection washed over him. He was reminded of a challenging time during his seminary days when he was assigned to a fieldwork church. The memory of that period was vivid, marked by unexpected adversity.

The church pastor had suddenly resigned, leaving the congregation in a state of uncertainty and disarray. Still a seminary student, Terrance found himself thrust into a leadership role he hadn't anticipated. The weight of responsibility was immense, and he felt the pressure of guiding a community through a turbulent time.

Terrance recalled the sleepless nights spent in prayer and contemplation, seeking guidance and strength. He remembered the initial fear and doubt, wondering if he was capable of stepping into such a significant role. But he also remembered the support he received from the congregation, their willingness to rally together and face the challenges head-on.

Through that experience, Terrance learned the true essence of leadership. It wasn't about having all the answers or never making mistakes. It was about being present, listening, and fostering a sense of unity and purpose. He discovered the power of prayer and resilience in himself and the community he served.

Reflecting on that time, Terrance felt a renewed sense of determination. He realized the adversity he faced then had prepared him for such moments. The lessons he learned in the seminary, the strength he found in his faith, and the support of those around him were all guiding him now.

With this reflection in mind, Terrance addressed the congregation once more, his voice filled with conviction. "Friends, as we move forward, we need to ensure our vision aligns with God's purpose for Calvary Church. It's not just about new programs or fresh ideas. We need to remain open to divine inspiration every step of the way."

Though still tinged with the tension of earlier conflicts, the room began to fill with a shared sense of purpose. Terrance felt a deep connection to his faith and a clear sense of purpose, which bolstered his confidence. Despite the hurdles, he believed in the path they were forging together and was resolved to see it through.

Glancing at Beth, while holding a sleeping 4-month old Grant, offered him a reassuring smile, Terrance felt a surge of gratitude and strength. Her quiet encouragement was a constant reminder that he was not alone in this journey. With his team's and the congregation's support, he was ready to lead Calvary Church into a new chapter, guided by faith and a commitment to their shared vision.

Merle nods sagely, his weathered hands folded on the table. "Amen to that, Pastor. We're building on holy ground here."

Terrance continues, his brown eyes alight with passion. "Remember the words of Proverbs 16:3: 'Commit to the Lord whatever you do, and he will establish your plans.' We must trust that our efforts, guided by His wisdom, will bear fruit in due time." Terrance can't help but reflect on the challenges ahead as he speaks. He feels a surge of hope, believing that even the most reluctant hearts can be softened with patience and faith.

As the meeting drew to a close, Terrance could sense the lingering tension in the room. He knew that the congregation needed more time to reflect and pray about the path ahead. With a calm and steady voice, he addressed the members once more.

"Friends, I appreciate your engagement and the heartfelt concerns you've shared tonight," Terrance began. "Given the weight of the decisions before us, I believe it's important that we take some time to reflect and pray about our direction. Let's use this time to seek God's guidance and ensure that our vision aligns with His purpose for Calvary Church."

The congregation nodded in agreement, understanding the need for thoughtful consideration. Terrance announced that the vote would be postponed until the next Voter's meeting in three weeks, giving everyone the opportunity to contemplate the proposed initiatives.

In the days that followed, Eleanor, Henry, and Jack decided to come together and offer a different ministry plan. They recognized the importance of presenting an alternative vision that addressed their concerns and resonated with other members of the congregation. The trio worked diligently, meeting regularly to develop their proposal.

As the next Voter's meeting approached, the atmosphere within Calvary Church was one of anticipation and hope. The congregation was eager to hear the new ideas and engage in meaningful discussions about the future of their community. Terrance and his core team remained open and receptive, ready to listen and collaborate.

With faith and determination, the members of Calvary Church prepared to come together once more, united in their commitment to seeking God's will and building a stronger, more connected community. Terrance knows that the outcome will not only define the church's future but also test the strength of its community. He steels himself, ready to face the challenges ahead with unwavering determination.

The following day, tension unwinds as Terrance discovers this quiet corner of respite. The room feels different with Merle as if the air is filled with calm and certainty. Terrance wonders how one man's presence can change so much, easing the burden of expectation with a nod and a gentle smile.

"It's been quite the start to the week," Terrance begins. "The meeting, Eleanor . . ." He pauses, shaking his head as if trying to clear the jumbled thoughts that refuse to settle. "I'm not sure I'm doing this right, Merle. Maybe I was too ambitious. Too soon."

Merle is the kind of listener who absorbs every word, showing the patience of someone who has experienced so much. His journey the corporate worlds is a familiar path, filled with stones and roots that can stumble those who aren't careful. "Every young leader has those feelings," he shares. "And honestly, some of us older ones do, too."

Terrance chuckles, feeling relief. Merle's honest words comfort him, reminding him he's not alone in this journey. "You have a way with words," he responds, his voice warm with gratitude. I have no idea how you held it together all those years!"

Merle's eyes crinkle at the corners, reflecting a wisdom gathered over the years. "I didn't," he admits, leaning in with a playful whisper. "I just let everyone believe I did."

They connect in a meaningful moment of quiet camaraderie, a wonderful meeting of minds that beautifully bridges the generational gap between them. Terrance feels comfortable sharing his thoughts, feeling unburdened by the need to put on a brave face. "It's harder than I anticipated," he admits. "The resistance, the pressure, and the fear of losing everything can be overwhelming."

Merle nods thoughtfully, feeling the weight of the younger man's words echoing his own past experiences. "Fear can be a powerful force, Terrance, but so can faith. Don't forget what you shared with the congregation this morning—God will give us the strength we need to carry on." Merle's voice brought Terrance back to what truly matters in his mission. In the eyes of the retired CEO, he sees a reflection of his own struggles, and he discovers a map, a guiding light, and a promise that he, too, can brave this storm with resilience.

"You have a wonderful vision, Terrance! That's exactly why you're here. It's also why some of them might feel scared," Merle adds. "Just remember, don't let that fear be louder than your call."

Terrance feels the truth of these words settling within him, grounding him. "I needed this," he admits, the weight of his gratitude filling the room with warmth. "Thank you for staying, for being here. For everything."

Merle's smile radiates warmth. "You're not alone, Terrance. You never have been, and you won't ever be. Remember that."

The conversation winds down, but its effect lingers, a soothing balm on the raw edges of Terrance's uncertainty. He stands to leave, feeling lighter and more sure of his path. The old man's words are a melody that plays in his mind, a tune of hope and assurance that fortifies his resolve. He heads back to the church, the anticipation of the coming weeks no longer a burden but a challenge he is ready to embrace. Merle watches him go, a knowing look in his eyes, and Terrance is reminded of the long road ahead and the strength he now feels to walk it.

The next steps are clear, and Terrance's heart is as steady as his stride. He knew what he needed to do to move forward and began to outline his next steps.

First, he decided to connect with Eleanor, Henry, and Jack. He understood the importance of addressing their concerns personally. "I need to reach out to them individually," Terrance thought. "I'll arrange one-on-one meetings to listen to and understand their perspectives better." He knew that building bridges and finding common ground was essential for fostering unity within the congregation.

Next, Terrance realized he needed to look into the history of Calvary Church. "Researching our church's history will help me frame the upcoming Voter's meeting in a way that resonates with our values and traditions," he mused. He planned to delve into Calvary's roots, past challenges, and successes, incorporating historical insights into his presentation. Highlighting how past experiences can guide our future decisions will provide a sense of continuity and reassurance to the members," he thought.

Finally, Terrance knew he had to prepare thoroughly for the next Voter's meeting. "We need to refine our proposal and address the concerns raised during the previous meeting," he decided. Terrance and his core team would ensure that the initiatives were well-thought-out and aligned with the congregation's needs. "Engaging the congregation through discussions, prayer sessions, and informational gatherings will help build support and foster a sense of collective purpose," he concluded.

With these steps in mind, Terrance knew that by connecting with key members, understanding the church's history, and preparing thoughtfully for the next meeting, they could navigate the challenges ahead and move forward with faith and unity. Glancing at Beth, who offered him a reassuring smile, Terrance felt a surge of gratitude and strength. Together, they were ready to lead Calvary Church into a new chapter.

Discussion Questions

Understanding Criticism

1. What are the primary concerns and criticisms raised by attendees during Terrance's town hall?
2. How did Terrance ensure that he fully understands the perspectives and emotions underlying these criticisms?

Effective Communication:

3. What strategies did Terrance employ to communicate effectively with his critics without escalating tensions?
4. How did Terrance show active listening and empathy during these interactions?

Addressing Concerns:

5. What steps should Terrance take to address the specific concerns raised by his critics?
6. How did Terrance prioritize and respond to the pressing issues raised during the town hall?

Building Trust:

7. How can Terrance rebuild trust with the community after a combative town hall?
8. What steps can Terrance take to demonstrate his genuine commitment to addressing the concerns of his critics?

Long-term Solutions:

9. What long-term strategies can Terrance adopt to prevent future conflicts and enhance relations with his critics?
10. How can Terrance engage the community in decision-making processes to ensure their voices are heard?

Personal Reflection:

11. How should Terrance reflect on his behavior and approach during the town hall?
12. What lessons can Terrance take away from this experience to enhance his leadership and communication skills?

7

Tears and Fears

"One factor can make or break your relationship when you are in conflict. That factor is attitude."

Relationships are Key

> The importance of maintaining relationships during the organizational change process is highlighted through interactions with key members. Successful change requires understanding and addressing the emotional and historical connections individuals have with the organization. By empathizing with their concerns, acknowledging their contributions, and involving them in the decision-making process, leaders can build trust and foster a sense of unity. These efforts demonstrate that preserving and strengthening relationships is crucial for navigating change and ensuring the organization remains cohesive and resilient.

Pastor Terrance returns to the office the day after Eleanor gets up and walks out after the highly charged and divisive meeting. Terrance slumps at his desk, too weary to pretend he's not. Terrance is struggling alone in his office with the weight of his responsibilities and the expectations of his congregation. Eleanor Davis's critique is that he is moving the church too quickly, and she shares with others that this is a church, not a business. She has said that the church often moves like a mighty turtle, slow with intentionality. Her words have hit him hard, especially when he feels overwhelmed and exhausted. He pushes aside half-drawn plans, scribbled sermons, and a much-avoided letter to Beth, letting his heavy head sink into folded arms. Last night was a blur. Grant's cries at two a.m. The failed delivery of yet another sermon. The stricken eyes of his most loyal parishioners.

The incongruous sharpness of Eleanor Davis's critique: "Just too worldly, Pastor. We are a church, not a business; these moves seem trendy, not nearly spiritual enough." Words he cannot keep pretending not to hear. He sits back up and finds his Bible beneath a mess of highlighted names and unanswered questions. Holds it like it can somehow shield him from the growing chaos. But can he really protect the church from going the way of all his scattered papers? In a rare moment of clarity, he scribbles an itinerary for the day. Meet Eleanor first. Then Henry. Then Jack. Makes a note to see Merle on his way home. He writes it all down, then stares, too tired to rub his eyes. He is exactly one man with two hands and far too little strength. God will have to do the rest.

He stands, stretches, and stares out the window where morning light filters softly, falsely, through the mist. The street is quiet and grey. An older couple walks hand in hand, a single-mindedness in their step. The church is their destination; of this, he is sure. He presses a palm against the windowpane. It is cool to the touch. Beth calls him on the cellphone, tells him Grant is fed and asleep again, and asks how long before he'll be home. He hears the waver in her voice, knows it's too much to ask of her, and knows they are unraveling faster than he can pull the threads back together. He calls a reply. "Late," he says, then again, softer: "Late." It echoes in the empty office. His own tired voice.

An answer, of sorts, comes. Let it be enough. Terrance hops in the car off to Eleanor's house.

It's Eleanor's ornate house rising tall and Victorian from the tangle of newer, cheaper homes that grew up around it. He pauses to admire the elaborate gardens, manicured with the same steadfast devotion she applies to everything, including faith. Snapdragons line the pathway like sentinels as he approaches the door. He's convinced himself it will be a good, productive visit—that Eleanor will open her arms wide, gather him in, and share in his burden.

"Thank you for visiting, Pastor," Eleanor says, her tone formal yet not unkind. "I trust you are finding Oakridge to your liking?"

Her words echo the expectations of an entire community. Terrance nods, buoyant as ever. "Very much so, Mrs. Davis. The town and the church have been incredibly welcoming."

She seems pleased with this response, folding her hands like a seamstress securing a delicate stitch. They move to the sitting room, a place where time seems reluctant to pass. Eleanor's steps are precise, guiding them past the watchful eyes of ancestors forever framed in sepia tones. The room is a mausoleum of heirlooms—every piece speaks to tradition, every corner whispers of the past.

"Please, let me pour you some tea," Eleanor offers, her formality softening slightly as she lifts a pot from a silver tray. Steam curls from delicate china cups, and she hands one to Terrance with steady reverence.

He takes a sip, savoring the warmth and the moment. "You have a beautiful home," he remarks, genuinely awed by the layers of history surrounding him.

"It has seen many seasons," Eleanor replies, a touch of wistfulness threading her words. "Much like Calvary Church."

A silence fills the room, dense and waiting. Terrance senses the shift as Eleanor stands and moves to a polished bureau, her steps slower now, as if wading through years of memories. She opens a drawer and retrieves a letter, yellowed with age and folded with care.

"There's something I wish to show you," she says, her voice tinged with something more than nostalgia. "This letter—it explains much of why I am as I am."

Her hands tremble ever so slightly as she hands it to Terrance, who receives it with the curiosity of one entrusted with an ancient secret.

"It was written during Pastor Klaus's time at Calvary," Eleanor begins. He once wrote, "Some feel I've come on too strong. Let those with ears hear. The future is not for the timid." Victor Klaus, the visionary who ran before the ink was dry on his call documents, was the radical they loved for eighteen brief, explosive months.

"My father wrote this in response," Eleanor says. Her own hand now. Perfectly looping. Composed. "My heart grieves for our Calvary, torn asunder. Our membership is divided and broken." She looks up and meets Terrance's gaze. He can see the emotion in her eyes, raw despite all the years. "I found it in his desk after he died. Pastor, it took years to heal those wounds. Some families never returned."

"Klaus wanted to change everything, to bring the church into a new era. It was all so . . . aggressive and no matter how much my dad tried to work with him. Klaus never backed down, and the conflict continued to simmer. My family tried to rally around my dad, supporting him through his recovery. Despite the tension, my dad remained committed to his role in the church, hoping that Klaus would eventually see reason. However, Klaus's vision for change was relentless, and he continued to push his agenda, causing further strain.

As months passed, the church community began to feel the effects of the ongoing conflict. Some members sided with Klaus, believing in his vision for modernization, while others stood by my dad, valuing the traditions and stability he represented. The division within the church grew, and it became clear that a resolution was needed.

In a bid to find common ground, a special meeting was called, bringing together key members of the church to discuss the future. My dad, despite his weakened state, attended the meeting, hoping for a breakthrough. Klaus presented his ideas with fervor, but my dad countered with a plea for unity and understanding.

The meeting was tense, with emotions running high. It was a pivotal moment for the church, and everyone knew that the outcome would shape its future."

She pauses, the word hanging in the air like an accusation, then softens as she sees Terrance's earnest attention.

"We lost nearly half our members that year. Families who had worshipped together for generations stopped speaking to each other."

Her voice quivers, betraying the vulnerability beneath her stern exterior. Terrance's eyes meet hers, and he sees more than a guardian of tradition; he sees a woman who has lived through the fractures of faith and family.

"That must have been incredibly painful," he offers gently, feeling the weight of her sorrow. "I'm beginning to understand your concerns."

Eleanor's gaze wavers, a flicker of gratitude sparking in her eyes. "I love Calvary Church, Pastor. I don't fear change itself. I fear what change might cost us."

Despite her wariness, there is a strength in her that he has overlooked. He watches it now, softening like an ice cube shrinking slowly in her steaming tea.

She sighs. "I don't want to see Calvary broken again, Pastor. Not in my lifetime."

He imagines Eleanor at his own funeral, comforting Beth with stories of the man he once aspired to be. "He meant well, but . . ." What? What can he possibly say? His words are stolen by her gravity. His thoughts are leaden with the burden he knows he must somehow make her share. He sees her waiting for a response. He is not used to seeing her wait.

"Eleanor, I understand your fears," Terrance begins, his voice steady but filled with empathy. "Calvary has been through so much, and the scars of the past are still visible. But I believe in our community's resilience. We have the strength to heal and grow stronger together."

Eleanor's eyes soften, and she nods slightly, acknowledging his words. "I hope you're right, Pastor. It's just that the memories are so vivid. The pain was real."

Terrance reaches out, placing a comforting hand on hers. "We will honor those memories, Eleanor. We will learn from them and ensure that Calvary remains a place of unity and hope. Together, we can build a future that respects our past but isn't bound by it."

She takes a deep breath, her resolve strengthening. "Thank you, Pastor. I needed to hear that."

Terrance leaves Eleanor's place, feeling he understands her stance more deeply. It has less to do with tradition and more to do with protecting Calvary from further trauma. One down, two to go. Terrance is off to the hardware store and an audience with Henry.

Terrance steps into Jenkins Hardware and feels the shock of noise and light. His presence was announced by the clanging bell, the abrupt turn of heads, the blaring music, and the sharp smell of sawdust and ambition. He was not ready for it, for any of it. Not for the change in pace, in sound, in power. Certainly not for Henry's startled glance from behind the register, his head snapping up as Terrance enters. But here it all is, undeniable and loud. Men are buying their way through lists of weekend projects. Paint brushes. Plywood. Nails by the pound. He watches the swift exchange of cash and goods and sees how it energizes Henry in a way that talk of innovation and change never quite seems to. It is just one more thing he has not prepared for. He's determined, though. Determined to understand. To close the gulf between the registers and the pews. He waits patiently, watching Henry thrive in his element, waiting to catch him the moment he is off guard. The moment he can catch him alone.

They exchange looks as Henry finishes with a customer. He acknowledges Terrance with a nod, the briefest sign of fellowship, before diving back into the day's work. Another customer demands his attention. Then another. The cash register rings. The radio blares. The phone trills. So different from the sacred silence of the sanctuary. So much urgency. It's an urgency Terrance can appreciate, even if it's one he cannot quite keep up with. The bustling energy of a man on a mission. He recognizes it in himself and knows that passion is current all too well.

Minutes pass. Terrance's confidence wanes. He begins to question the wisdom of this strategy, this ambitious showing up unannounced. It's been Henry's way all along. The best defense is a strong offense. Silence and endurance from the back row of the sanctuary. Surprised him once today. Perhaps he should call it a victory, regroup, and surprise him again tomorrow.

The pace shifts and slows. Henry's shoulders relax and settle into their natural, authoritative state. An old man in flannel shuffles toward the register, three screws cupped in one gnarled hand. He catches Henry's attention with a subtle nod and a knowing glance in Terrance's direction. He will be back, the look says. He's a patient man. With a small salute to Terrance, he sets the screws on the counter and makes his way out. The day is yours.

A sudden solitude surrounds them.

"Well, I'll be." Henry's voice booms over the quieting clatter. "You don't see this side of town very often, do you, Pastor?"

Terrance is quick to recover, quicker than he'd thought he'd be. "Needed to see the source of that collection plate," he says. His own words, for once, surprised him. "Didn't know it would be so bright and noisy."

Henry's laugh is half cough, half thunderclap. It rings through the shop. "Man's work should never be quiet, Terrance." He is still the only one who ever calls him that. Terrance is beginning to understand why.

"It's good to see you, Henry." He steps forward and holds out a hand. He feels the power of Henry's grip, the strength that the years have not yet managed to whittle away. "Do you have time?"

"Don't get many days off." He scans the store, making sure he isn't needed, making sure the pews and empty silences of the church haven't somehow found their way into the store to cramp his employees' style. "But for you, I'll make an exception." A pause. "This time."

Terrance follows him through the aisles, past shelves of plywood and hammers, plumb lines and plans. An entirely different ministry. They wind up in a cramped office at the back of the store. It's as cluttered as Terrance's own. More so, perhaps. Invoices instead of sermons, filing cabinets instead of Bibles. He eyes a cardboard box filled with ledgers. It is marked, in thick black marker, RECEIPTS. The word is underlined three times. He is not sure if he wants to laugh or cry.

"Sit down, sit down," Henry says, gesturing toward an old metal chair. Terrance pulls it up, grateful for the rest, grateful to have caught Henry at all.

The old man has already pulled two Styrofoam cups from a stained stack, and is already pouring coffee from a battered thermos. "You look like you need it."

Terrance thanks him, takes the coffee with the same gratitude. Feels the heat through thin, cheap foam. "This is an impressive place, Henry."

"Hard work." The words are almost an accusation, almost a benediction. "But I'm not telling you anything you don't already know." He shifts his gaze to Terrance, eyes narrowing. "How's the little one?"

"Loud," Terrance says. "He's…a blessing."

"Ah, the double-edged kind," Henry says, though there's warmth in his voice, a brightness Terrance has never quite heard from him before.

"Yes," Terrance says, the closest thing to an agreement they've had in months.

Henry leans back in his chair. Behind him, an old clock ticks out the silence. Terrance counts each measured moment, waiting for the pivot, waiting for the sudden shift of energy, for Henry's inevitable repositioning. There is the sense, though, that he is already a step ahead, that he has prepared this space, these words, long before Terrance thought to barge in on his business. He lets the tension linger, lets it build.

"I'm assuming you're here on official business," Henry says at last.

"Not entirely," Terrance says. "Wanted to hear more about how you got this place up and running."

"Well, I don't have the thirty years it'll take to tell you." There's no bitterness in the words. Just fact, pure and simple.

"You could give me the short version," Terrance says. "That way, we can both save a little time."

"Short version, huh?" He drains his coffee and leans back in his chair again. "Here it is. Man comes back from Korea. Has nothing but a GI Bill and a baby on the way. Works construction, odd jobs. Gets tired of making money for everybody else. Puts his nose to the grindstone and builds a place of his own. Slowly." He points to a framed photo on the wall behind him. The store on opening day. Old pickup truck in the lot, ribbon across the door. Faded paint on the windows. Bold letters: GRAND OPENING! CONGRATULATIONS HENRY! "They thought I'd last a year."

"Who did?"

"Everyone."

"And how long?"

Henry takes a sip of his coffee. Pauses. "How long have you got?"

There's a world behind the words. Years of toil and struggle. Terrance hears them all and knows the commitment, the tenacity it must have taken. Knows the dogged determination and the driving need. "It's an impressive place," he says again, this time more slowly. He means it.

Henry's eyes gleam with satisfaction. "Like I said. Hard work."

"So's ministry," Terrance says, measuring his words as carefully as Henry measures his own. "This is why I needed to see you."

The pivot. The shift. A lifting of weights.

"I know," Henry says.

"You don't think this is sustainable," Terrance says, hearing the truth of it in Henry's pause.

"Not if we blow the place up. There's such a thing as too much change, Terrance. We're in the red. If you think we can spend our way out, you're not the businessman I thought you were."

He reaches beneath a stack of papers and pulls out the spreadsheets Terrance had forgotten all about. Even Eleanor has left him reeling. They are numbers the color of his eyes: blue. Cold, piercing, logical, they lay bare the truth of it.

"I've never been a businessman," Terrance says, half an apology, half a boast.

"And I'm not a pastor," Henry says. "Though I do have some insight." He points to the spreadsheets, the hard numbers, the dire straits. "We've lost a third of our income over the past decade. People are not tithing like they used to. You want us to put in screens and update the sound system, hire a new youth minister, convert the old meeting space into a multi-purpose area? I have a better idea. Why not sell it all and start over in a basement somewhere?"

"We'd lose people," Terrance says.

"We're losing them now. Let's not lose everything, too." His voice is the same as always. Commanding, clear. But there's a note of something else, a lower, sadder register. There's a wistfulness, a fragility Terrance has not heard before.

"I know you don't agree with my approach," Terrance says. "But you do care, don't you?"

"If I didn't, I'd be out there making money right now." He gestures toward the front of the store, toward customers who are too busy to worry about God, salvation, eternity. Too busy buying and building and thriving. It is a business that should be none of Henry's, but it weighs on him just the same. "You'll learn. You've got time." The words, half promise, half challenge. "Here. Let me show you how it's done."

He reaches into a desk drawer, scribbles something on a notepad, tears the page off, and slides it toward Terrance.

"What's this?" Terrance picks up the note and squints. 15% CONTRACTOR DISCOUNT, it says. Even the number is the color of his eyes. He's not sure how to read it, how to interpret the offer, how to let it reshape all his preconceptions.

"I do have some insight," Henry says again.

A glimmer of unexpected hope. Terrance feels his spirits rise and sink just as quickly. Hope is the one thing he should never doubt, the one thing he should always possess in abundance. He is young, he is idealistic. He knows this, accepts it as his greatest strength, his greatest liability. "Thank you, Henry. I mean it." The words are earnest and measured. He stands, holds out his hand again. "I'll see you Sunday?"

"We'll see," Henry says, gripping Terrance's hand with surprising gentleness. There is something there. Maybe more than something.

He steps out into the daylight, the sharp shift of noise and light, the sudden return of activity. More customers. More energy. More cash in the till, and maybe, if God wills it, more cash in the offering plate, too. He will let it take time. He will let the letters turn red, black. He will let the weeks stretch out into months, into years. He will let them stretch out into eternity if he has to.

But he hopes to see Henry Sunday, just the same.

Terrance feels hopeful as he forms deeper relationships and connections one conversation at a time. Eleanor provided an insightful historical context. Henry provided a businessman's perspective. He is not opposed to change but he sees everything through the lens of an Excel spreadsheet. Next is Jack. This meeting may be the most difficult of them all. He sees Calvary through the eyes of the loss of the love of his life.

The diner throbs with life, an artery of conversation and clattering dishes, but the booth where Terrance sits across from Jack Whitmore is an island of tension. Vinyl creaks as they settle in, both men ordering coffee and sizing each other up like rival contenders. Jack's posture is a fortress, his arms folded tight and his gaze as steely as the silver napkin holders on the table. Terrance leans forward, trying to bridge the chasm between them with a smile that's both sincere and hopeful. Their words start off stiff, strangers forced to share the same unsteady ship.

"So, Pastor," Jack begins, his tone as rigid as his stance, "what brings you here?"

Terrance senses the undercurrent of accusation but chooses a path paved with optimism. "I thought we might clear the air, Mr. Whitmore."

Jack nods, his movements economical and controlled. "I suppose you've heard about the petition."

Terrance nodded, maintaining his calm demeanor. "Yes, I have. And I want to understand your concerns better. This community means a lot to me, and I believe we can find a way to move forward together."

Jack's eyes narrowed slightly, but he remained composed. "It's not just about the petition, Pastor. It's about feeling unheard and overlooked. Many of us feel that our opinions don't matter."

Terrance took a deep breath, choosing his words carefully. "I hear you, Jack. And I apologize if my actions have made anyone feel that way. Let's take this opportunity to discuss specific issues and find solutions. I want to ensure that everyone feels valued and included."

Jack's eyes survived the diner before his eyes settled back on Terrace. "Alright, let's start with the decision-making process. We need more transparency and involvement from everyone."

Jack's demeanor softens, he feels like for the first time he is being heard. The conversation went deeper. "Pastor, I appreciate your efforts, but Calvary... it's not the same without Dorothy. She was the heart of this place for me." Now we are getting to the heart of Jack's real issue.

Terrance feels the weight of Jack's grief. "I understand, Jack. Dorothy's presence is deeply missed by all. Her spirit and kindness touched everyone."

Jack's eyes welled up with tears. "She believed in Calvary's mission, in its ability to bring people together. But now, I struggle to see that vision without her."

Terrance moves closer, his tone empathetic. "Jack, Dorothy's legacy lives on in the community she helped build. Her love and dedication are woven into the fabric of Calvary. We can honor her memory by continuing to foster the unity and compassion she cherished."

Jack takes a shaky breath, his emotions raw. "It's hard, Pastor. Every corner of this place reminds me of her."

Terrance places a comforting hand on Jack's shoulder. "We will walk this path together, Jack. Calvary's strength lies in its people; together, we can find a way to heal and move forward. Sarah's vision can still guide us."

Jack nods slowly, a glimmer of hope in his eyes. "Thank you, Pastor. I needed to hear that."

Terrance smiles, "We're in this together, Jack. Always. Let's work on creating a more inclusive process. Your feedback is crucial, and I want to make sure we build a stronger, more united community."

By the end of the meeting, there was a sense of cautious optimism. The road ahead wouldn't be easy, but with open communication and mutual respect, they believed they could overcome the challenges together. As they share a moment of understanding, Terrance sees a way to bridge the divide and accomplish a new shared vision for Calvary. Each conversation and connection brings him closer to rebuilding the unity and hope that Calvary once embodied.

Terrance heads over to meet Merle. He had so much to share.

Merle Thompson's colonial home is a testament to tradition and transformation, its stately columns embracing change with dignified grace. Terrance parks his car in the wide gravel drive, noting the seamless blend of past and present in the architecture. Inside, Merle ushers him into the study. Their conversation begins with the warmth of shared tea and polite pleasantries, but Terrance knows from the set of Merle's features and the intent in his eyes that their meeting will soon wade into deeper waters.

"Welcome, Pastor," Merle says, his voice resonant with the authority of one who has both led and followed. "I've been looking forward to our chat."

His handshake is firm, and his bright eyes seem to instantly assess Terrance. He leads the young Pastor into the study, where certificates and awards glint modestly from the walls, quiet testaments to a life of accomplishment.

"Quite a collection you have here," Terrance remarks, "I can see why some might think of it as a second church."

Merle chuckles, the sound rich and full. "It's been called that, among other things. Please, have a seat, and let's get comfortable."

They settle into chairs that flank a low table, a pot of tea steaming between them. Merle pours with the precision of a man accustomed to measured actions and thoughtful planning.

"How's Beth and little Grant?" Merle inquires, his interest genuine and warm.

"Doing well," Terrance replies, smiling at the thought of his young family. "Beth keeps everything running smoothly."

"Behind every good pastor," Merle says with a knowing nod. "And how are you finding our little corner of the world?"

"It's been both challenging and rewarding," Terrance admits, feeling the openness of the moment. "I came here with big dreams, but I'm learning to appreciate the wisdom of experience."

Merle leans back, a glimmer of satisfaction in his eyes. "Experience is just mistakes made long enough ago that they finally seem like wisdom. You've come to the right place, Pastor."

He reaches for a binder, its edges worn from use, and opens it to reveal a diagram charting the emotional stages of organizational change. Terrance leans in, drawn by Merle's clarity of vision and confidence of expression.

"People don't resist change," Merle explains, tracing a line with his finger. "They resist loss."

Terrance takes in the words, the simplicity of the statement resonating with his own recent struggles.

"Families, churches, companies," Merle continues, his voice steady and assured. The principle remains consistent. The key is fostering relationships while creating a compelling future vision. This approach strengthens connections and inspires a shared journey toward what lies ahead.

His hands move with the grace of a conductor, orchestrating the complex symphony of human emotion and organizational strategy. Terrance watches, captivated by the ease with which Merle navigates these waters.

"Every merger, every transition," Merle elaborates, pulling out sheets filled with detailed plans. "I've found that if people see where they fit into the future, they'll be more willing to let go of the past."

The room is a gallery of successes, each framed with an award and certificate that testify to Merle's lifetime of dedication. Terrance sees not just the tools of a career but the echoes of a calling that parallels his own in unexpected ways.

"I'm beginning to see why they called you the king of corporate America," Terrance says, his admiration unfeigned. "But it sounds like the heart of your work was never just business."

Merle nods, his expression thoughtful. "You can't lead people without loving them. It's as true in the boardroom as in the sanctuary."

The insight lands like bulletin board material, offering Terrance a profound and practical perspective. He feels the old man's words stitch together a pattern of understanding, including Calvary Church's history and hopes.

"I think I've made some mistakes," Terrance confesses, his voice tinged with the vulnerability of new wisdom. "At the town hall, I might have pushed too hard, too fast."

Merle studies him. The pause is pregnant with the weight of both challenge and encouragement. "Mistakes," he echoes, "are just new opportunities wearing yesterday's clothes."

The sentiment sparks a smile from Terrance, who sees in Merle not just an ally but a kindred spirit.

"We need to reconnect with folks like Eleanor and Henry," Merle advises with his profound and straightforward strategy. "Bring them into the conversation. Let them know they're heard."

The young Pastor nods, the path before him clearer now than ever since his arrival in Oakridge.

"That's a road I'm willing to walk," Terrance replies, feeling the promise of Merle's support like a firm hand at his back.

They talk long into the afternoon, their conversation a rich blend of spiritual insight and strategic planning. The air is thick with the aroma of hope, a sweet counterpoint to the tea that has grown cold in their cups.

As the meeting winds down, Merle places a hand on Terrance's shoulder, the gesture as grounding as the prayer that follows.

"Lord," Merle intones, his voice both humble and powerful, "grant Pastor Terrance wisdom and courage as he shepherds us through this time of change."

Terrance bows his head, feeling the swell of gratitude for the guidance and friendship this man of vision and heart extended. He leaves the house with renewed confidence, the echoes of Merle's prayer and the strength of his insights fortifying his every step.

Driving away, the road unfurls like a bright ribbon, leading him toward a future that honors the traditions of the past and the necessary transformations to come.

Tears and Fears

As Terrance leaves Merle Thompson's impressive colonial home, feeling renewed purpose and direction, he decides to reconnect with his wife, Beth. He dials her number and hears the familiar sound of her voice, filled with warmth and concern. Terrance shares updates from his meetings with Eleanor, Henry, Jack, and Merle, detailing the insights and progress. Beth listens attentively, but her voice carries a hint of weariness as she mentions that their son, Grant, has been fussy and missing his dad. She admits that she, too, misses her partner and wonders when he will be home. Terrance reassures her that he will return soon, expressing his gratitude for her support and understanding.

This conversation reminds him of the importance of balancing his responsibilities to the church with his commitment to his family, reinforcing his resolve to navigate the changes ahead with empathy and care.

Terrance, aware of how much time he has spent on this change process, agrees that these are the last three stops before some much-needed downtime with Beth and Grant. He is off to the music studio to meet with Oliver and Jimmy.

The music studio is a cathedral of sound, its walls lined with instruments that hang like sacred relics. Terrance meets Oliver Williams and Jimmy Rodriguez here, among the tangles of recording equipment and the ghosts of half-finished songs. Their initial enthusiasm is muted now, dulled by the aftermath of the town hall confrontation. Oliver's usual vivacity is subdued, his laughter less frequent, while Jimmy sits with the contemplative air of a man tuning an off-key piano. Terrance begins to share insights from his meetings with Eleanor, Henry, and Jack, and his words create a new melody that he hopes will bridge the gap between past aspirations and future possibilities.

"Didn't think we'd see you so soon," Oliver jokes, but his voice lacks its usual exuberance. "Thought we might have scared you off."

Terrance smiles, unshaken by their dampened spirits. "It'll take more than a town hall to keep me away."

Jimmy nods, his warm brown eyes fixed on Terrance. "The storm needed to come, Pastor. Sometimes, the air only clears when the rain has fallen."

Terrance takes a breath, the weight of recent conversations filling his words with new depth. "I wanted to share where things stand and how some unexpected doors are opening."

Oliver leans in, curiosity fighting the pall of doubt. "Do tell."

"Folks like Eleanor, Henry, and even Jack—they're beginning to come around," Terrance explains, his voice carrying the conviction of newfound hope. "I think there's a real chance to build something that includes everyone's vision."

Jimmy's smile is slow and knowing, like a sunrise. "Bridging generations through shared harmony. Sounds like music to my ears."

The metaphor lands softly, a balm to their discouragement. Oliver's eyes brighten, and his infectious enthusiasm stirs from its slumber.

"Does that mean we'll see more of the classics alongside the new stuff?" Oliver asks, his tone shifting from skeptical to intrigued.

"Exactly," Terrance confirms. "We're looking at ways to honor our rich heritage while still reaching new families through worship and new ministry initiatives. The future is more than just music. It is about forming new relationships."

Oliver grins, the familiar spark reigniting. "Now that's a concert I'd like to play."

Their renewed enthusiasm hums in the room like an unstruck chord waiting for the right moment to resonate. He leaves them in a better mental space than after the meeting. There are a few more stops on the way home.

Terrance next finds himself at Carolyn and Jonathan Mitchell's home, where the aroma of freshly baked cookies weaves a warm welcome. The couple greets him with kindness and reservation, their soft eyes reflecting trust and uncertainty.

"Pastor," Carolyn says, ushering him inside. "We're so glad you could stop by."

"Thank you for having me," Terrance replies, taking in the cozy surroundings. "It's good to see you both."

They settle around the kitchen table; the air is fragrant and inviting, but Terrance senses the lingering echoes of doubt from their last meeting.

"We were worried," Jonathan admits, his voice a gentle rumble. "The meeting at the church—it was quite a shock."

Terrance nods, the memory of that stormy night still vivid. "I know it was hard to hear. But I've been listening, and I want you to know that your concerns are important."

Carolyn pushes a plate of cookies toward him, the gesture more than mere hospitality. "And do the others feel the same way?"

Terrance takes a cookie, its sweetness counterpoint to the challenges he faces. "I think they do. Folks like Eleanor and Henry—they've been through this before. Their insights have been eye-opening."

Jonathan leans forward, his silvered hair catching the afternoon light. "You're really bringing them into this, then?"

"Absolutely," Terrance assures, his tone resolute. "We need everyone's voice if we're going to build a church that honors the present and future."

Carolyn's expression softened, and the weight of the past weeks lifted. "That means a lot to us, Pastor."

Her eyes meet Jonathan's, a silent understanding passing between them. "Then we're with you," he says, the commitment in his words as solid as the love that binds them.

They part with renewed determination, the cookies half-eaten and the doubts more than half-resolved.

Terrance's next stop is Sarah Chen's design studio, where blueprints and fabric swatches form a tapestry of creativity. She greets him with the keen gaze of an architect, seeing the bones of a structure beneath its surface.

"Pastor Terrance," Sarah says, her voice both welcoming and precise. "Come in, please. You've caught me between projects."

The studio is a flurry of design elements, contrasting Sarah's calm and methodical presence.

"I'm glad you had time to meet," Terrance responds, taking in the artistic chaos surrounding them. "I wanted to update you on how things are shifting."

Sarah motions for him to sit, her hands in constant motion as she clears a space. "I've been following the developments. Tell me how I can help."

Terrance outlines the renewed vision for Calvary, including the surprising collaboration with those who once seemed opposed. Sarah listens, her sharp mind piecing together the strategy like a well-designed blueprint.

"Incorporating their perspectives could strengthen the foundation," she observes, her voice analytical yet warm. "Are they really on board?"

"I believe they will be," Terrance answers, encouraged by her insights. "We've started conversations, and they're more open than I ever expected."

She nods a quick, decisive moment. "It sounds like you've built quite the coalition."

"Thanks to a lot of support," he replies, gratitude and determination blending in his voice. "With your help, I think we can truly transform Calvary."

The meeting concludes with Sarah's pledge of support, her enthusiasm as tangible as the architectural plans that fill the room.

Terrance returns home, where Beth and Grant are excited to see him. He is energized by the weight of these new alliances, crystallizing into a concrete plan. The paper in front of him fills with names and sketches of a leadership team that now includes Eleanor, Henry, Jack, and all his original supporters.

The vision of Calvary's future becomes clear, a blueprint for transformation that marries tradition with necessary change.

He leans back in his chair, gently rocking Grant to sleep while reflecting on the journey that brought him to this moment. The challenges and triumphs of the past weeks converge into a single, hopeful path forward.

Terrance feels the momentum of collaboration, the energy of a community united by shared faith and renewed purpose. It's a sweet harmony, the beginning of a new song that promises to carry Calvary into a bright and vibrant future.

Discussion Questions

Eleanor Davis' Perspective:

1. As Eleanor shared, how can understanding the church's history help address current fears and resistance to change?
2. What strategies can be employed to humanize and address the fears of change within the congregation?

Henry Jenkins' Entrepreneurial Insight:

3. How can Henry's financial acumen and business perspective be leveraged to benefit the church's transformation?
4. How can church leaders balance financial considerations with spiritual and community needs?

Jack Whitmore's Emotional Connection:

5. How can church leaders support members like Jack, who view the church through the lens of personal loss?
6. What role does empathy play in bridging divides and fostering collaboration within the church community?

Merle Thompson's Guidance on Change Management:

7. What are the key insights Merle shared about managing change and strengthening relationships?
8. How can church leaders apply these insights to reconnect with emotionally shaken core team members?

Collaborative Efforts and Vision for the Future:

9. How did the meetings with Oliver, Jimmy, Carolyn, Jonathan, and Sarah contribute to a renewed collaboration and vision for Calvary's future?
10. What steps can be taken to ensure the expanded core team, including Eleanor, Henry, and Jack, remains cohesive and focused on the church's transformation goals?

General Reflection:

11. How can one-on-one meetings, like those conducted by Pastor Terrance, be used effectively to build deeper relationships and connections within the church community?
12. What are the potential challenges and benefits of forming an expanded core team to lead the church's transformation?

8

From Conflict to Community

"Learn from the past. Prepare for the future. Live in the present. Those unaware of their history, origin, and culture are like trees without roots."

The Leadership Factor

> Leadership is crucial in uncertain and turbulent times. It remains steady despite cultural shifts, changing ministry challenges, and organizational stagnation. Leaders must take charge and guide the organization to effective change. Analyzing organizational change in churches requires examining leaders' roles and effective leadership styles.

Terrance and Beth get up early and take their morning walk with Grant in the stroller. They use this time to catch up on the current information from family and friends and connect as a couple. When they return from their walk, Beth wishes Terrance a good day at the office, reminding him of the love and support waiting for him at home. Terrance heads off to his office, feeling grounded and ready to navigate the upcoming changes with empathy and unity. This is reinforced by key church community members' insights and perspectives.

As he settles into his prayers, he reflects deeply on the conversations and insights gained from his recent meetings.

Terrance's mind drifts to Eleanor's yellow letter detailing the conflict between Pastor Klaus and Eleanor's father. Terrance leans back, letting the letter rest gently on the polished wood. The early morning light casts shadows across the room, transforming the scattered pages into ghosts. He imagines the elderly man at his desk, pen trembling with each stroke, heart growing weary with every word. Eleanor's father had feared for the church's soul, having seen it slip through his fingers. In his efforts to save it, his own life slipped away. His heart attack came swiftly after Klaus's removal, a cruel punctuation mark at the end of a lifetime of service. Eleanor never forgave the man who shattered her world. Her bitterness ran deep, staining the years with its stubborn permanence. The letter vividly reminds Terrace of the deep historical wounds within the church. It emphasizes the importance of acknowledging past conflicts to avoid repeating mistakes"

Terrance pauses and rises from his desk, crossing the room with the letter still grasped in his hand. The church's history envelops him like an ancient mural, with every brushstroke narrating tales of faith and struggle. Eleanor's pain, he realizes, is not merely a solitary wound. It is a thread that weaves through generations, linking her to a legacy she cannot escape. Her father dedicated himself to Calvary Church, shaping its traditions with the sweat of his brow and the beat of his heart. Eleanor grew up within this sacred fortress, every stone a testament to her heritage. She stands now as its guardian, protecting it with a passion fueled by love and fear.

Forgiveness, he knows, is a radical act of faith, a surrender to divine love that transforms and renews. He thinks of Jesus on the cross, his words resonating through the ages: *"Father, forgive them, for they know not what they do (Luke 23:34)."* Redemption, Terrance realizes, is not just for the offender but for the wounded, offering freedom from bitterness and the chance for rebirth.

His mind turns to the congregation and the fractured relationships that echo Eleanor's pain. He sees the path forward with a clarity he didn't have before. To lead is to heal, to bind together what history has torn apart. Understanding the past is essential, but living in it is a slow suffocation. He recalls Paul's words: *"Forgetting what lies behind and straining forward to what lies ahead, I press on (Philippians 3:14)."* It is a call to move, to change, to live anew. But how does he bring Eleanor along without losing her to the shadows that cling to her feet?

He then thinks of Jack's emotional revelation about losing his beloved wife, Dorothy. Jack's pain highlights members' personal connections with church traditions, and Terrance understands that changes can feel like losing another loved one. This realization underscores the need to approach transitions with sensitivity and empathy.

Jimmy and Oliver's energy and passion inspire Terrance. Their enthusiasm for contemporary worship motivates him to blend modern elements with traditional ones, creating a vibrant and inclusive environment that appeals to all generations.

Terrance then considers Carolyn and Jonathan's steady, quiet support. Their reliability and understanding of members' emotional attachments to church traditions remind him of the importance of dependable allies. Their support is crucial for bridging the gap between different perspectives within the congregation.

Terrance recalled the discussion with Merle. The elder statesman of the church said. "What you're trying to build won't stick without relationships." His words were like smooth stones dropped into still water. Terrance nodded, feeling those words ripple through him, unsettling and profound. He knows the divide is more than just history. It's personal, and healing requires more than time.

Merle's presence resembles an ancient clock ticking steadily, marking moments with measured patience. He gazes at Terrace with eyes that have witnessed too much to rush. "People need to feel they belong," he continues, his tone gentle yet firm. "If they don't, they'll drift away like leaves in the wind."

Terrance absorbs Merle's wisdom, its gravity pressing it into him. He sees relationships in Scripture, the bound love between Jonathan and David, and the trust that held the early disciples together. But Merle's advice imparts a weight and texture that rings differently.

"I suppose I've been focusing too much on what," Terrance admits. "And not enough on who."

Merle nods, a subtle gesture that conveys much. Without people, ideas lack the support to thrive. Relationships are the lifeblood of, and the very heart of change."

Merle's wisdom resonates strongly with Terrance. Merle explained that people resist loss and do not change, and shared strategies for maintaining strong relationships during periods of growth and transition. Terrance reflects on the importance of honoring the past while painting a compelling picture of the future.

Eleanor, Henry, and Jack—names that loom large, each carrying their own scars and hesitations. Terrance realizes their resistance is not just to novel ideas but to letting go of a community they no longer recognize. His initial approach, though sincere, was too much about transformation and not enough about preservation. He needs to understand, connect, and become part of their world.

"Finding common ground is like tuning a fine instrument," Merle says, a twinkle in his eye. "Sometimes you have to play more than one note."

Terrance smiles, but Merle's words press on him like a challenge he must meet. His mind flashes back to the stories he read about Eleanor's father and the agony the change caused. If relationships are the key, he has much to learn and build. "It's deeper than just history, isn't it?" Terrance asks, leaning forward, seeking the clarity Merle seems to possess.

Merle's answer is slow and deliberate, like a map unfolding: "People don't just cling to the past for the sake of it. They cling to it because it holds their identity, their belonging."

"How do I bridge that?" Terrance asks, his voice eager and apprehensive.

Merle said, "You're doing it right now." You're asking. You listen. Keep it up, and they'll hear you, too."

The simplicity of Merle's advice felt profound, like the first light of dawn after a long night. Terrance's mind races with possibilities, and the enormity of the task threatens to overwhelm him. But Merle's calm, his steadfast certainty, was like an anchor. It kept Terrance grounded and focused.

"Their legacy," Terrance murmurs, almost to himself rather than to Merle, "and their fears. That's where I need to connect with them. I want to help them feel that they truly belong," Terrance shares, his voice filled with heartfelt determination. "They are an important part of this, not in spite of the change, but because of it!"

"Then you have a good start," Merle replies, rising slowly, his movements as deliberate as his words. "Just remember, son, change isn't the enemy. Disconnection is."

He vows silently to include Eleanor, Henry, and Jack—both new and old, skeptical and hopeful. He will not only lead them but will also walk alongside them. He will serve as a bridge, linking them as they cross into the future.

Eleanor smooths her skirt and sits, her resolve as tightly wound as the curls in her hair. Around her, Calvary's committee assembles, some eager, some uneasy, all ready for their say. It feels like the first day of school, Terrance thinks, surveying his gathered students of tradition and change. In place of textbooks, the table holds hastily copied agendas. Instead of a bell, the soft chiming of Carolyn's silverware summons them to order. There is a sense of anticipation mixed with the scent of fresh-baked bread—a kind of excitement and hunger.

Terrance stands, his usual warm smile adding brightness to the room. "Thank you all for being here," he begins, his voice full of conviction. "Our mission is to reach those who feel disconnected, and I'm excited to hear your thoughts on how we can make Calvary a welcoming home for everyone."

The room settles into focus, eyes shifting to the papers and then to one another. Carolyn's dining table, sprawling and wooden, seems to grow with each new idea, each whispered prayer for guidance. Eleanor feels it stretching across the room and generations, and she wonders how far she can stretch with it.

Eleanor clears her throat, feeling the weight of expectation from the eyes around her. "Perhaps," she starts, her voice faltering but firming, "perhaps we could create a space inviting young families. Somewhere, their children feel they belong."

The suggestion hangs in the air like a tentative note. Surprise registers on the faces around the table, mingling with curiosity and cautious optimism. Oliver's grin is wide and immediate. Henry, caught off guard, furrows his brow, but Eleanor sees something that doesn't just doubt in his eyes. It's the first hint of openness.

"It's a wonderful idea," Terrance says, beaming at Eleanor. "What does everyone think?"

A murmur of agreement rolls around the room. Sitting with hands folded like a patient architect of change, Agnes nods her approval. "Building for the future," she says with a soft smile. "That's always a wise investment."

Like gentle rain, her words soak into even the most resistant hearts. Henry shifts in his chair, arms crossed but loosening. "A playground, maybe?" he suggests, and it's as though an unseen barrier falls away with the quiet hum of his voice. Jack looks at him with surprised respect, which breathes something new into both of them.

Encouraged, Terrance captures the room's collective enthusiasm. "So let's be bold in our plans," he says. "Who wants to take on the task of organizing?"

From Conflict to Community

Jonathan and Carolyn exchange a look full of silent communication and mutual support. Carolyn speaks, her voice as warm and inviting as the home she's made around them. "Why don't we meet here? I can't promise you won't gain a few pounds, but it's always open."

The laugh she draws feels like a shared heartbeat, bringing them closer, a single family in a single room. Terrance agrees, thanking Carolyn and Jonathan for their hospitality. "It's perfect," he says. "We can make this a real team effort."

Agnes gives Eleanor a reassuring look. "You've surprised us today," she tells her, and Eleanor feels an unexpected lightness, like something has shifted within her, like a gate swinging open.

The conversation swells, punctuated by the clink of teacups and the sound of forks meeting plates. New voices enter the mix, unfamiliar yet welcome. Jimmy and Oliver, both with easy camaraderie and wide gestures, invite fresh faces into the discussion.

"Don't be shy," Jimmy encourages his teacher's instinct to nurture evident. "Every idea counts."

The new members, some unchurched, some young and searching, add a vibrancy that enriches the dialogue. "What if we have music nights?" one suggests. Another, inspired, offers, "And movie screenings! Open to the whole community."

Oliver's enthusiasm is boundless, his laughter like a bridge spanning the space between generations and beliefs. "That's the spirit," he says, and the new suggestions ignite a fire in the others.

Eleanor watches Henry and Jack, feeling the current of excitement drawing her in. She senses their grappling with uncertainty and a willingness she hasn't seen before. "And what do you think, Henry?" she asks, her tentative tone and knowing.

He takes a moment, his booming voice measured but sincere. "I think we should give it a try," he finally admits, looking at Jack, who nods in agreement. It's a small sentence but carries the weight of commitment, an anchor now light enough to lift.

Terrance, sensing progress, decides to press ahead. "A community night," Terrance suggests, his words lifting like steam from a fresh cup. "We can show them what this new vision looks like." Carolyn nods, thinking of food. Oliver thinks of music. Jimmy thinks of every friend he can invite. This is a moment of momentum; each person catches it like a child catching the tail of a kite, like a prayer.

Terrance's excitement is infectious. "It's an opportunity to demonstrate what Calvary can be," he continues, passion dancing in his eyes. "Let's make it something everyone wants to be part of."

Agnes folds her hands, her quiet presence commanding attention. "What about those who've drifted away?" she asks. "Can we bring them back to the fold?"

"We'll need a strong lure," Henry says, and his booming voice holds a note of reluctant eagerness. "Something they can't ignore."

Carolyn smiles, already planning menus in her mind. "Good food usually does the trick," she offers. "Jonathan and I can handle that."

"And music," Oliver adds, leaning forward, his voice like a chord of possibilities. "Something fresh and alive."

The energy in the room crackles, each suggestion building on the last like a crescendo. Jimmy's thoughtful voice rises above the enthusiasm. "Let's include activities for everyone," he proposes. "We can show them a taste of the new Calvary."

The ideas flow, vibrant and varied, as though the Holy Spirit is present in every thought. Jonathan joins in, suggesting crafts for kids and games for teens. Still riding the wave of her boldness, Eleanor throws out another idea. "How about a trivia contest?" she says, and the room erupts in agreement. Even the skeptics can feel the pull, the warm current of the community sweeping them along.

Terrance watches with gratitude, amazed by the transformation taking place before his eyes. "We need a name," he says, wanting to capture the spirit of this moment.

"Together in Faith," Carolyn suggests, and its simplicity and truth silence the room. Heads nod. It's a name that speaks to them all, that wraps around each person like an embrace.

"Let's make it happen," Terrance concludes, dividing the tasks. Carolyn and Jonathan on food and activities. Oliver and Jimmy on music. Sarah, though quiet, volunteers for decorations, using her eye for detail and balance. Beth jumps in, offering crafts and games for the younger crowd. Henry and Jack agree to handle invitations, their voices mingling in a way that surprises them both. Every hand is raised, and every heart is ready to contribute.

Terrance led the gathered mass in a table prayer, thanking God for the food and fellowship. Dishes were spread across long tables like patchwork, every one a small offering. Beneath them, tablecloths ripple in the evening breeze, a sea of food ready to sail. As Terrance says amen, "Dig in," someone calls, and Calvary's congregation closes ranks, forks raised. Children sprint for the mac and cheese, their faces decorated from the day's adventures. Henry stands by with a full plate and an even fuller smile as if this feast is one he's waited for all his life.

The potluck is a masterpiece of sharing and community. Platters of roasted chicken, casseroles crusted with golden breadcrumbs, and salads dotted with vibrant colors beckon to the hungry crowd. There are plates of cookies and pies at the far end, a sweet promise waiting to be fulfilled. The aroma of home-cooked meals fills the air, mingling with laughter and the soft hum of conversation.

Groups gather around tables, forming circles of connection. Longtime members mix with newcomers, their dialogues as rich and varied as the food before them. "Pass the cornbread," someone calls, and the simple act of sharing stretches smiles and bonds alike.

Eleanor sits with Agnes and a group of children, her stern exterior softened by the light of the occasion. "You won't leave room for dessert!" she warns, watching with amusement as young hands grab for another helping.

In another corner, Oliver's casual and lively voice carries over the din. "That's a killer bean dip," he exclaims, and even those who've held back from the new vision find themselves drawn to the warmth of his exuberance.

The evening continues in a gentle swirl, each new connection a thread weaving through the tapestry of Calvary's fellowship. Carolyn and Jonathan float among the guests, offering refills and encouragement, their presence a testament to the love they've invested in this community.

"Jimmy, what did you bring?" Oliver teases, eyes on the carefully wrapped tamales.

"Mi abuela's recipe," Jimmy replies, and the mention of his grandmother, a nod to heritage, speaks volumes to the journey they're all embarking on.

The joyful sound of children fills the spaces between bites. Even the littlest ones, sitting cross-legged on the floor, are part of the gathering; no one is left out or forgotten.

As plates empty and the sun dips below the horizon, Oliver and Jimmy take their places. Soft and compelling music rises, a hymn of unity that echoes the heart of the event. The choir joins in, their voices a mix of old and new, tradition and change. Some songs are familiar, wrapping around the congregation like an old shawl; others are fresh, stirring souls with their unfamiliar beauty.

Eleanor, ever the guardian of stories, stands with purpose. She has planned this moment, and the others recognize the strength and intention in her step. "Time to share what really matters," she announces, and members take the floor one by one.

The stories begin slowly, words like gentle rain falling onto fertile soil. A young couple talks about finding faith when they'd thought it lost. An older man, his voice breaking, tells of the years when he felt alone and the day that changed. These narratives of hope and struggle pull tight and true as the listeners weave themselves into the tellers' journeys.

Tears mingle with laughter as more voices join, each story a step closer to one another. In sharing their histories, they build their future, laying a foundation of trust and understanding.

Terrance watches, his heart full, as connections deepen. He sees Eleanor and Henry in conversation, and their animated expressions suggest a friendship that was never expected, a blessing still unfolding. He sees Jack laughing with a young family, the lines of resistance on his face smoothed by grace.

As the night deepens, the conversations continue. It's as if no one wants to leave, no one wants to break the spell of unity that has wrapped around them. Members of Calvary linger, some speaking quietly, others already planning their next steps in this shared journey.

In the aftermath of the evening, as the hall slowly empties, a profound sense of purpose remains. It lingers like the scent of warm bread, like the echo of a joyful song. The new vision for Calvary feels close, as tangible as the embrace of friends, as promising as the stars that begin to prick the night sky.

Optimism rides high as the community reflects on the transformation they've witnessed. What seemed impossible only weeks ago now feels inevitable. They have shared a meal, a song, a story, and a vision together.

People are putting together care packages for the local homeless shelter in another corner of the building. Cards spread like flower petals on a spring day, and eager hands pluck them from the floor. "To the residents," Jack instructs, his voice like a coach, like a new tradition. Members of Calvary gather around him, pens raised and ready. Outside, others work at filling packages with toothpaste and shampoo as if the small acts will wrap the town in grace. As if they already have.

Jack stands at the helm, directing with a purpose that lights a fire in those around him. His previous skepticism seems worlds away, replaced by a dedication that echoes through his words and actions. "Let's make sure each card is personal," he urges, passing out stacks like an eager vendor on a crowded street.

Henry, beside him, adds his booming encouragement. "This is what we're about," he proclaims, and his voice carries with it the weight of commitment, of a future he's ready to embrace.

Groups form, clustering around tables and on the floor, each a small colony of industry and intent. Beth gathers a young group, her calm demeanor guiding them with a steady hand. "What do you think they need most?" she asks, inviting them to see beyond themselves.

Jimmy and Oliver, in another corner, provide their usual spark of energy. They've brought unchurched friends along, and their enthusiasm is contagious. Even those new to the community find themselves drawn into the effort, pens flying, packages filling.

"It's like a choir," Jimmy says, and his eyes crinkle with the joy of the metaphor. "Each person adds their voice, and together it sings."

Laughter punctuates the work, and there is a rhythm to the collaboration. A joyful noise rises from the mundane work of assembly and organization. It speaks of unity and purpose, of lives intertwined in service.

Outside, a crowd tackles the bulkier tasks. Large boxes fill with the promise of care, and even the littlest hands play a part, their contributions small but mighty.

Henry stands back, surveys the scene, and smiles a deep, satisfied smile. "We're making an impact," he tells Jack, his words carrying more than simple observation. They carry the weight of hope and belief.

Jack nods his expression, a mixture of awe and determination. "And we're just getting started," he replies, his voice full of the thrill of new beginnings.

The congregation joins in, drawn by the lively atmosphere and the call to action. What started as a project became an event, a celebration of shared mission and vision. It's as if the town itself has heard the invitation and opened its hearts wide to accept it.

Each finished card and filled package speaks of the church's broader goals, each a small echo of Terrance's new vision. They are tangible reminders of Calvary's commitment to its members and those yet to come.

In the midst of the activity, Carolyn and Jonathan pause to take it all in. "Look at them," Carolyn says, her voice tinged with amazement. "Look at us."

Jonathan squeezes her hand, and the moment of connection mirrors the broader one that enfolds the congregation. "It's happening," he agrees, and his quiet words carry the certainty of faith rewarded.

The event winds down with an atmosphere of fulfillment and excitement. The cards are stacked, the packages sealed, and the room is filled with the unmistakable scent of success. What started as small acts of service has grown into something far greater, something as expansive and encompassing as love.

For Terrance, the sight is nothing short of a revelation. He sees the evolution of the church in every interaction and every act of service, and his heart swells with the joy of witnessing a community truly coming together. They have taken the first steps, bold and brave, towards the vision he so desperately hoped they could embrace.

As the crowd disperses, there is talk of what comes next. "We should do this more often," someone suggests, and others chime in with ideas and possibilities, the buzz of enthusiasm electrifying the air.

Terrance listens, knowing they are ready to bring this new vision to the wider congregation. They have shown what is possible, and the project's success sets the stage for the next chapter in Calvary's story. A chapter they will write together.

The last blush of the sun fades into the horizon, and a ring of faces glows in the encroaching dusk. Voices, softer now, murmur like a river at rest. "Let's bring it all together," Terrance suggests his words the night's refrain. He leads them to a circle, hands joined, heads bowed. Silence blooms, then gives way to a prayer so full it lifts them like a benediction.

"Thank you, Lord, for this community," Terrance begins, his voice carrying strength and humility. "For the love and the hope you've planted here tonight."

The prayer is both a plea and a praise, winding through the assembled like a golden thread. Each person feels its touch, and each responds with silent affirmation, a whispered amen, a gentle squeeze of the hands they hold.

As the prayer concludes, they linger in the circle, reluctant to break the spell of togetherness. The twilight air hums with the warmth of shared purpose and the comfort of common dreams.

Eleanor is the first to speak; her voice is a minor miracle of change. "I never thought . . ." she trails off, searching for words that elude her. "I never thought it could be like this."

"You mean wonderful?" Agnes offers, her eyes twinkling with wisdom and mirth.

Henry's laughter rumbles through the gathering, more a revelation than a sound. "I have to admit, I was wrong," he confesses, his words met with good-natured jibes and knowing smiles.

"It wouldn't be the first time," Jack quips, nudging him with a companionable elbow. The ease between them suggests more than newfound camaraderie; it suggests lasting change.

The reflections spill out, each one a testament to the power of the evening. Young and old, new members and lifelong ones, all find their voices in the dusk, speaking a language of hope and renewal.

Oliver's bright and irrepressible laugh punctuates the conversation. "Look at us, talking like one big family reunion," he says, and his words hold the truth of the night.

Conversations splinter into smaller, intimate groups, the glow of faces lit now by the enthusiasm of ideas and the promise of more to come. They discuss the success of the event, how it exceeded their expectations and solidified their path forward.

"We've planted the seeds," Carolyn remarks to a cluster that includes Sarah and Jonathan. "Now we just have to keep watering them."

"And pull the weeds," Jonathan adds, his gentle humor a balm.

Across the circle, Terrance listens, heartened by the optimism and unity he sees in every interaction. His own journey has been a winding road of doubt and faith, but tonight, it feels straight and sure, guided by the steady light of conviction.

The committee members come together, buoyed by the night's success and eager for what's next. "We need to update the congregation," Agnes suggests, her tone suggesting both the task and the joy it will bring. "They should hear how far we've come."

"And see where we're headed," Terrance agrees, imagining the path as he speaks it into being. "We have our next Voter's meeting in a week. We need to put together an official proposal. We can present the new vision for Calvary and show them everything we've worked for."

"After this," Eleanor states with newfound confidence, "they won't need much convincing."

The group's readiness and excitement are electric, a testament to the transformation they've all experienced. What began as a seed of hope has grown into something large enough to hold them all, a vision vast and inviting.

As the evening winds down, the reflections turn to farewells, and each goodbye is filled with the certainty of more hellos, gatherings, and shared dreams. The night may end, but its spirit stretches into the future, endless and alive.

Terrance stays behind as the crowd slowly dissipates, taking a moment to stand in the quiet echoes of the hall. It's a place that held uncertainty and doubt only weeks before. Now, it has the possibility of being rich and ready. He thanks God for the grace that brought them here and the promise to carry them further.

He joins Beth and Grant, whose silhouettes wait in the doorway, warmed by the glow of shared triumph. Together, they leave the church, the night and its memories wrapping around them like a cloak.

Anticipation courses through Terrance are like a hymn. The event's success is the proof he and the church needed. With renewed strength and confidence, they are ready to present this new vision to the wider congregation, share what they have witnessed, and invite all of Calvary to be part of it.

The horizon seems bright with expectation, and Terrance sees a path wide and welcoming in that expectation. It is a path they will walk together, bold in faith and alive with hope.

Discussion Questions

Understanding Eleanor's Past:

1. How does Terrance's discovery of Eleanor's father's letter enhance his understanding of her resistance to change?
2. What impact does learning about Eleanor's father's untimely death have on Terrance's approach to leading the church?

Roles and Responsibilities:

3. How did they ensure that each committee member's unique gifts were utilized effectively?
4. What strategies did they adopt to encourage more members to assume leadership roles?

Embracing Change:

5. What compromises have we made in the past, and how have they benefited our church community?
6. How can we continue to cultivate a culture of openness toward new initiatives and change?

Creating a Welcoming Atmosphere:

7. How can we create Carolyn's warm and welcoming environment in other church settings?
8. What role does hospitality play in encouraging open dialogue and engagement?

Engaging the Unchurched:

9. What are some effective ways to invite friends who do not attend church to church events?
10. How can we make sure their perspectives are heard and valued in our discussions?

Vision for Ministry:

11. What are the key elements of Calvary's new vision for ministry, and how do they address the needs of young families and marginalized individuals?
12. How can we effectively convey this vision to the wider congregation?

Community Event Planning:

13. What activities and elements should be included in the "Together in Faith" event to ensure it strengthens bonds and fosters unity?
14. How can we measure the success of this event in terms of community engagement and unity?

Food and Fellowship:

15. How does sharing food help foster a sense of community?
16. What other activities can we include to enhance fellowship during church events?

Storytelling and Testimonies:

17. How can we encourage more members to share their personal faith stories?
18. What impact do these stories have on fostering connections and empathy within the congregation?

Community Service:

19. What other community service projects can we undertake to highlight our commitment to serving others?
20. How can we engage more members in these projects to promote a sense of mission and unity?

Reflection and Prayer:

21. How can we foster more opportunities for reflection and group prayer within our church activities?
22. What are some ways to ensure that these moments enhance the sense of community and gratitude?

9

Guided Through the Wilderness

"Wonderful things happen when people's spirits are strong, focused, and vibrant."

Collaboration

> Collaboration is a powerful force in organizational change. When individuals come together, pooling their diverse skills, perspectives, and experiences, they create a dynamic environment where innovative solutions can flourish. This collective effort fosters shared ownership and commitment, making the transition smoother and more effective. Team members can address challenges more comprehensively through collaboration, leveraging each other's strengths to overcome obstacles. It also builds trust and unity, as open communication and mutual support become the foundations of change. Collaboration transforms organizational change into a collective growth and achievement journey. This ensures that the organization emerges stronger and more resilient.

Terrance stood before Calvary Church, surveying the upturned faces with swelling gratitude. This made him grip the pulpit tighter. His breath felt like a prayer in his chest, sacred and poised to spill over, taking flight like an army of birds. The old pews creak beneath with an eager quiet. In the third row, Eleanor pursed her lips, a determined look on her face. This was as if she prepared to tackle challenges with unwavering strength. Jack sat to her left on an island of calm. Near the back, Oliver's energy vibrates like a tuned fork. Terrance pauses, thinking: "God is in the midst of our mess. For a moment, the whole year telescopes inward—all the heartbreaking uncertainty and miracles, together in a dizzying blur—and then resolves into something truly unforgettable and whole.

The silence is a wide-open sky, Terrance's voice a gentle ascent. "This past year, we have walked a challenging path," he begins, meeting their eyes with the warmth of a shared secret. He sees Henry with his steadfast gaze and Carolyn leaning into Jonathan, their hands knitted together like the fabric of faith. Terrance sees stories unfolding in these faces—testimonies of doubt, fear, surrender, and hope. He breathes in, feeling the sacred gravity of the moment. "We faced conflicts that threatened to pull us apart," he continues, inviting them to remember and bear witness. "But through it all, God's presence was our guiding light. We have seen His hand in every situation, no matter how messy."

His voice grows as he shares their journey, unspooling like a thread that stitches them together. "I stand before you thankful for how far we have come. The sermon today is titled 'God amid Our Mess,'" he says, letting the phrase rest among them like a stone dropped into still water, rippling outward. "As Romans 8:28 reminds us, *'And we know that in all things God works for the good of those who love him, who have been called according to his purpose.'*" Terrance sees Oliver's lips moving with the words, repeating them like lyrics to a familiar song.

He felt the pull of their past, the tension and the struggles, like chords waiting to be resolved. "When I first arrived at Calvary Church, I sensed your pain," he says, his voice softening as if cradling a fragile thing. "There were disagreements, and our hearts were heavy. There was tension because of our dire financial situation. Your previous shepherd retired, and this young rookie is brimming with creative ideas and change. The committee meetings often felt more like battlegrounds than places of fellowship." He let the weight of those memories linger, drawing a breath that reached every corner of the room. "But even in the thick of the conflict, God's love was at work." Jesus was present in every argument and tear, guiding us toward something greater than we could see."

The congregation is still expectant. Even Eleanor appears ensnared by the sincerity of his words, her usual sternness melting away into a more tender expression."We faced opposition," Terrance continues, "but God's presence was undeniable. Jack, Eleanor, Henry—your willingness to listen and compromise was a testament to His hand at work." He sees Jack smile, serene and knowing, a lighthouse in the fog of doubt. "By proposing new initiatives and working together, you showed that God's grace is bigger than any division."

Terrance allows the story to unfold, his words weaving their collective history. "Carolyn and Jonathan," he says, nodding to where they sit, a gentle anchor in a sea of uncertainty. "Your hospitality and warmth created a space where dialogue could happen. You showed us that when we open our homes and hearts, unity is not just possible—it is inevitable." Carolyn's eyes glisten with the brightness of new understanding, reflecting the spirit that fills the room.

"And let's not forget the fresh perspectives that brought us new life," he says, his voice lifting with the joy of new beginnings. "Jimmy and Oliver—your courage to invite those outside our church family brought insights we never imagined." Oliver beams, his enthusiasm spilling over like a dam broken wide. Jimmy nods in quiet affirmation, his experience demonstrating the power of diversity.

Terrance breathes in the complexity of life, marveling at the intricate design that God has carefully crafted together. "Through the process, we have seen God take our mess and turn it into His message. We are living proof that His glory shines brightest in our darkest times." The words vibrate with the truth of what they have lived by, echoing in their hearts like a heavenly refrain.

Terrance looks over the faces of the congregation, alive with the appreciation that threads through him like golden light. His voice breaks through the waiting silence, each word a gift unwrapped and shared. "Our journey has been difficult," he says, "but God's hand has been upon us through it all." He speaks with the awe of a heart laid bare, telling them of their struggles. They nod, a sea of quiet agreement flowing into their story. His words breathe life into their past, turning struggles into landmarks of faith. They have made it through, each step marked by the miracle of grace.

Terrance felt their connection—an unbroken circle of understanding surrounding him like a warm embrace. "We began with tension between us," he recalls. His tone carried the heaviness of those early days. "Some said change was needed, while others feared what new trauma it might bring." His eyes find Eleanor and Henry, their unbending faces softening in recognition of their clash. "It felt like an impasse, but God had a plan we couldn't see." They look to him, eyes wide open with recollection and acceptance, as he describes the story of their shared trials.

"Faith became our guiding light through the darkness," Terrance continues, his voice steady with conviction. "It gave us the strength to face our fears and the courage to embrace change. In trusting that plan, we found the resilience to overcome our differences and grow together as a stronger community."

"Even in our strongest disagreements, God was at work," Terrance continues, "transforming adversaries into allies." Eleanor catches Henry's glance, their eyes meeting in a truce that speaks volumes. They are changed, not just in stance but in spirit. This proves what Christ-like love can do when it takes root and grows wild in the heart. Love has the power to bridge divides that seem insurmountable, bringing understanding and compassion where there was once only discord. It nurtures patience and forgiveness, allowing individuals to see beyond their differences and embrace each other's humanity. This way, love becomes a transformative force, healing wounds and fostering unity. "God leads us," Terrance adds, "through impossible moments, revealing His purpose and peace."

His words weave through the congregation like a melody they know by heart but love hearing anew. "Merle," Terrance says, his voice echoing reverence, "your wisdom led us toward compromises for the greater good. Your faith was an anchor in our storm." Merle smiles, a reflection of quiet humility and joy, knowing the strength it took to stand firm and let go all at once. The congregation listens intently, their faces a mix of awe and delight. Some nod in agreement, while others wipe away tears, touched by the authenticity and truth of Terrance's message. As the words settle over them, a sense of unity and renewed hope fills the room, binding them closer together.

"And in the end, our Together in Faith community event was a celebration of God's love," Terrance adds, letting the memory of that day saturate the silence. "We saw unity and fellowship bloom in ways we dared to dream but scarcely believed possible." He pictures the laughter, the shared meals, the stories that wove their lives together more tightly than they ever imagined.

"Community event became a beacon, drawing us closer to each other and those beyond our walls," Terrance continues, his voice colored with the joy of witnessing God's plan unfold. "And our worship, our storytelling—it was His love, alive and at work among us, bringing us to tears, to laughter, and to deeper connection."

He sees the faces before him, each one a living testimony to God's faithfulness. "Let us pray," he says, closing his eyes, feeling their hearts rise with gratitude and expectation. "Lord, thank You for Your steadfast love and guidance. Thank You for taking our mess and making it Your masterpiece. May we continue to see Your presence in all we do. In the precious name of our Lord and Savior Jesus Christ. Amen." The room breathes with him, the unity of their voices a whisper and a promise, binding them to the past, the present, and the glorious unknown that stretches ahead.

After the service, the core team assembles to present their slide presentation of the revised vision for Calvary Church.

Pastor Terrance stood before the congregation, his voice filled with enthusiasm, as he recounted the journey of developing Calvary Church's ministry plan.

"Dear friends," he began, "I am thrilled to share how our dedicated core group has come together to create a comprehensive ministry plan to guide us forward." Each member played a vital role in this process, and I am deeply grateful for their contributions.

With his remarkable financial planning expertise, Henry has been instrumental in crafting our budget. He meticulously outlined all the necessary expenses, ensuring every aspect of our ministry is accounted for. His work has given us a solid financial foundation, giving us the confidence to manage our resources effectively.

Our group has also been proactive in identifying and securing funding sources. Together, we have explored various avenues, including donations from our generous community, grants from charitable organizations, and support from local businesses. Seeing our team's determination and collaborative spirit has been truly inspiring.

Sarah Chen, known for her exceptional organizational skills, has volunteered to create a detailed ministry timeline and action plan. She has carefully mapped out each step, setting clear milestones and deadlines. Her structured approach ensures we stay on track and make steady progress toward our goals.

With her creative flair for design and technology, Rebecca Lawson has offered to craft a stunning digital presentation. This will be available for you and the entire community on our newly designed website. She envisions a captivating visual story conveying our vision and plans to the community.

As we work together, our core group's synergy and shared passion have become evident. We are not just planning but building a future for Calvary Church that will inspire and uplift our entire community. I am excited about what lies ahead and grateful for each member's dedication."

My vision for Calvary Church extends beyond our immediate plans. I dream of a church that offers engaging programs for young children, discipleship training to equip families to nurture their spiritual growth, and provides a safe, supportive environment. Specifically, we will have Sunday school classes, After-school tutoring, micro school space for homeschool families, Vacation Bible School during the summer, and a weekly Kids' Club where children can engage in fun, faith-based activities.

I envision a worship service that blends traditional hymns with contemporary music. This will create a harmonious and inclusive atmosphere where everyone can connect with God through His Word and music. Jimmy and Oliver, our talented musicians, will lead this effort. Jimmy will focus on traditional hymns, bringing his deep knowledge and passion for classical church music. Oliver will introduce contemporary worship songs, adding modern touches to our services. Together, they will create an engaging and uplifting musical experience.

Moreover, I see our congregation actively engaged in community outreach, making a tangible difference in the lives of those around us. We will host regular community events, including a food pantry to support struggling families and a ministry dedicated to helping the homeless. These initiatives will provide essential resources and compassionate support, embodying our church's love and care.

I picture our members getting deeply involved in these outreach events, living out our vision in meaningful ways. Volunteers will be the backbone of our food pantry, organizing donations, distributing food, and offering a listening ear to those who come for assistance. Our ministry to the homeless will see members preparing meals, providing clothing, and offering support and companionship to those in need.

Through these efforts, I believe our congregation will embody the spirit of service and compassion at our faith's heart. Each act of kindness, each moment of support, will be a testament to our commitment to living out the teachings of Christ in our daily lives. Over time, these initiatives will foster a stronger sense of community and belonging among residents, promoting a network of support and resilience. As relationships deepen and trust builds, individuals and families will feel more empowered to seek help and contribute to the well-being of others. Ultimately, these efforts will meet immediate needs and inspire a culture of generosity and compassion that will resonate throughout the community for years to come.

I am excited about what lies ahead and grateful for the dedication of each member. Together, we will build a church that serves its members and reaches out to touch the hearts and lives of many."

I want to request your support in approving this new vision plan. With your approval, we can move forward, united in our mission to serve and uplift our community."

The congregation voted, and a resounding 75% majority approved the proposed vision plan. Pastor Terrance and the church members ended the meeting on a high note, singing "Amazing Grace" together. Their voices were filled with hope and gratitude for Calvary Church's future.

Pastor Terrance felt excitement and anticipation after the congregation approved the new vision plan. The approval ushered in a transformative journey for Calvary Church, and the next steps were crucial to ensure the vision became a reality.

With his remarkable expertise in financial planning, Henry took the lead in finalizing the budget. He meticulously incorporated any last-minute adjustments based on feedback from the congregation, ensuring that every necessary expense was covered. His work provided a solid financial foundation, instilling confidence in the church's ability to manage resources effectively. The group then turned their attention to securing funding. They began actively pursuing identified sources, reaching out to potential donors, applying for grants, and engaging with local businesses for support. Their determination and collaborative spirit were truly inspiring as they worked tirelessly to gather the necessary funds.

Sarah Chen, known for her exceptional organizational skills, refined the ministry's timeline and action plan. She sets specific dates for each milestone and event, ensuring everyone stays on track and makes steady progress. Her structured approach was invaluable, keeping the group focused and motivated.

Rebecca Lawson, with her creative flair for design and technology, finalized the digital presentation. She incorporated additional information and feedback from the town meeting, crafting a captivating visual narrative that would convey the vision to the broader community and potential supporters.

The church began organizing programs for children with the foundational elements in place. Sunday school classes, Vacation Bible School, and the weekly Kids' Club were prepared to launch. Volunteers were recruited, and materials collected to ensure that these programs would nurture young children's spiritual growth in a safe, supportive environment.

Jimmy and Oliver, the talented musicians, started rehearsing and planning the blended music worship services. Jimmy focused on traditional hymns, drawing on his deep knowledge and passion for classic church music. Oliver introduced contemporary worship songs, adding a modern touch. Together, they created a harmonious and inclusive atmosphere where everyone could connect with God through song.

The church also set up the food pantry and ministry to the homeless. Volunteers were trained, and resources were gathered to ensure these initiatives could start helping the community as soon as possible. The congregation's involvement in these outreach events embodied the spirit of service and compassion at the heart of their faith.

Pastor Terrance and the core group held regular meetings to monitor progress, address challenges, and make necessary adjustments. They kept the congregation informed and engaged through updates and feedback sessions, fostering a sense of unity and shared purpose.

As the church moved forward, the synergy and shared passion within the core group became evident. They were not just planning; they were building a future for Calvary Church that would inspire and uplift the entire community. The journey had begun, and with each step, they were living out their vision in meaningful ways.

As Calvary's voters' meeting ends, Terrance and Beth take Grant for an evening stroll to get him to sleep. They reflect on how far God has brought them on this renewal journey. They feel a deep sense of gratitude and humility, recognizing the challenges they've overcome with faith and perseverance. As they look back on the journey, a sense of peace and accomplishment fills their hearts, knowing they have positively impacted their community. Their reflections are also tinged with hope for the future, eagerly anticipating Calvary's continued growth and renewal.

Beth squeezes Terrance's hand. "Can you believe how far we've come?" she whispers, her voice filled with awe. Terrance nodded, recalling the pivotal moment they organized the first community outreach event.

This brought together people from all walks of life. It was a turning point that ignited a new sense of unity and purpose within Calvary. This laid the foundation for the many initiatives that followed. "That day changed everything," he replies softly, a smile on his lips.

The event was filled with nervous excitement and determination as they watched the diverse crowd gather. There was an overwhelming sense of fulfillment as they witnessed strangers becoming friends and barriers breaking down with each conversation. Knowing their efforts planted the seeds of change and unity within the community was a moment of pure joy and validation.

Terrance nods, a smile tugging at his lips. "It's been a long road, but every step was worth it." Eleanor, Henry, and Jack were deeply committed to stalling and delaying the process. Despite their initial resistance, they eventually saw value in the outreach. Eleanor's skepticism about the event's impact became advocacy as she witnessed the community's response. Once doubtful, Henry and Jack became champions of the cause, helping bridge gaps and foster understanding across diverse groups.

As they enter the parsonage, they know this is just the beginning of an exciting chapter. Their efforts have strengthened the bonds within Calvary and inspired other communities to embark on similar journeys of renewal and unity. The ripple effect of their initiatives has the potential to create a legacy of collaboration and understanding that extends far beyond their immediate surroundings. As new leaders emerge and take up the mantle, the spirit of inclusivity and shared purpose will continue to thrive, shaping a brighter future for future generations.

The Key Elements in Making an Organizational Change Flourish

Clearly Define the Vision.

Recommendations

Given its size and polity, communication within the organization is a complex task. However, during the change management process, ensuring that the right message reaches the right audience at the right time is crucial. Effective communication, though time-consuming, cannot be overstated. It is important to remember that several audiences, including congregation members, staff, church board members, lay leaders, volunteers, and influencers, need to be addressed. Some churches have additional groups to engage due to their polity and structures, and we must not overlook the unelected influencers. Clear and inclusive communication is key to keeping everyone informed and involved.

Communicate, communicate, and communicate more when the organization encounters challenges. Churches can disciple and grow their leaders by providing clear directions, establishing accessible communication channels, and fostering a kingdom mindset. Avoiding the blame game and making immediate corrections strengthens the church culture and community.

It is crucial to remember that change often creates a sense of loss. Embracing empathy and recognizing that everyone is human is essential. Most people do not intentionally create barriers without good reason, such as seeking accountability or protecting their time. Instead of fostering conflict, communication from a place of understanding promotes empathy and clarity. This approach helps overcome internal barriers and makes everyone feel understood and valued in the change process.

Generate Short-Term Wins.

Recommendations

Planning and executing short-term wins require strategic thinking and focus. Leaders must understand how to generate a sense of urgency to create short-term wins. To achieve this success, a leader must overcome the tyranny of the urgent and focus on the more critical necessities that do not demand immediate attention. Celebrations are not just a formality; they sustain the team's morale and keep momentum.

Build on the momentum of change.

Recommendations

Entrenched practices can impede change in any organization. A complex web of interdependencies exists between them. One ministry program or committee must complete its tasks to achieve its ministry objectives. The church must reorganize these interdependencies to function effectively. Change can be slowed or even halted if outdated relationships are not addressed.

The church is in the final stages of the change process. At this point, it is easy to overlook the ministry's initiatives, culture, and outcomes, which would derail the essential actions needed to nurture the change vision. Acceleration is crucial for enforcing and maintaining the policies, systems, practices, and environments necessary to make the change vision permanent.

This stage is critical to the next and final phase of the change management process: implementing change. Change agents must identify issues within the church's structure or culture that hinder change at this stage. He notes that change is fragile until properly established. There is a risk that things will revert to their previous state until a new equilibrium is achieved.

Making the Change Stick.

Recommendations

Addressing the underlying culture and values is essential to anchor change moving forward. New paradigms must be introduced for organizational change to occur at the first-order level. An organization must embed innovative approaches into its culture and values to achieve second-order change. The church's mission must be deeply rooted and accountable to its members to foster buy-in and lasting commitment. Shepherds can achieve this by framing change within the congregation's global mission. God's mission is their "why." Pursuing one's calling to serve God and others is the essence of a good organizational purpose statement. Members are encouraged to be driven by a greater calling than personal gain. In addition to giving meaning to service, this approach evokes deeper connections and inspires individuals to act.

Discussion Questions

Town Hall Meeting:

1. How does the atmosphere in the fellowship hall during the town hall meeting reflect the congregation's shift towards unity?
2. What impact does the recorded vote of 70 percent in full agreement have on the church's future?

Role of Key Figures:

3. How do the contributions of Merle, Eleanor, Sarah, Oliver, and Jimmy illustrate the collaborative effort in revitalizing Calvary Church?

Evening Walk with Beth:

4. How does the quiet walk with Beth provide a moment of reflection and gratitude for Terrance?
5. What role does divine guidance play in their conversation about the church's journey?

Themes of Renewal and Unity:

6. How do the themes of renewal and unity manifest throughout the chapter, and what moments stand out as particularly significant?
7. What lessons can be drawn from the church's journey in balancing tradition with necessary changes?

Future Prospects:

8. How does the chapter's conclusion with Terrance and Beth feeling hopeful about the future set the stage for Calvary Church's continued growth?
9. What do you think are the key factors that will determine the success of Calvary Church's ongoing transformation?

kjhk

10

A Community Reborn

"Regeneration is necessary for every generation. The restoration, renewal, revival, reclaiming, and redemption of people is more important than anything else."

As the Easter morning light rises through the stained glass windows at Calvary Church it fills the day with hope and promise. Eager footsteps leave delicate patterns on the dew-kissed grass, while the early birds joyfully make their way toward the sanctuary. The pews come alive with friendly faces and anticipation, creating a sea of warm handshakes and joyful reunions. A kind middle-aged man with distinguished salt-and-pepper hair warmly leads a gathering of spirited souls, their hearty laughter and friendly embraces weaving a quilt of friendship and hope through the tranquil morning air. From across the lawn, a newcomer guides a lively group of widowers and widows, their steps light and filled with laughter. Inside, a youthful musician with shaggy hair casually slings a guitar over his shoulder, his enthusiastic strumming quickening hearts and kindling song. Before long, the air is filled with the joyful rush of melody as young and old blend their voices, their praises unfurling like a vibrant banner that simply reads: love.

Oliver Williams beams with enthusiasm, his fingers deftly navigating the strings, inviting the congregation to join him as he leads the blended choir. "This is for the next generation!" he exclaims, his voice carrying a joyful challenge. The opening chords of a contemporary worship song fill the air, echoing against the church's freshly painted walls. Faces around the room brighten, and voices rise to meet his.

A young father in the front row lifts his son onto his shoulders, both sharing in the exhilaration of the moment. Elderly members, hands arthritic yet determined, clap along, connecting the past with the present in a shared melody. A sea of expressions—some reserved, others jubilant—unite in a single act of devotion. The chorus swells, powerful and consuming, an offering of sound that echoes to the rafters.

In the children's ministry area, Carolyn Mitchell flits from room to room like a warm breeze, her curly hair bouncing with each step. "They're going to love this," she tells a fellow volunteer, her eyes sparkling with anticipation. The classrooms overflow with excitement as twenty children, eager and full of energy, pour in. Their laughter and high-pitched chatter create a spirit of innocence, echoing the church's renewal. Carolyn watches a toddler embrace a new friend, a bond formed in the cradle of shared playtime. A teenager takes a moment to assist a younger child, their interaction warm and natural. She savors this scene of unity, a mosaic of age and spirit that fuels her commitment. The church's newfound vitality reflects her own joy, a joy as expansive as her heart.

Meanwhile, across the hall in between services, Henry Jenkins stands at the center of a bustling men's Bible study group. His presence is both commanding and welcoming, his broad shoulders reflecting strength and resolve. The group surrounds him, a diverse mix of long-time members and fresh faces drawn from the wider Oakridge community. "Thank you, God, for this fellowship," Henry intones, his deep voice resonating with sincerity. The men echo his sentiment with a hearty "Amen," their connection palpable. He opens the Bible, his salt-and-pepper beard contrasting sharply with the vibrant cover. Laughter punctuates their rich and authentic study. Conversations ebb and flow, touching on scripture and life's challenges, mingling reverence with camaraderie.

"Remember when this was just a dream?" one member asks, nostalgia weaving through his words. Henry nods, the sparkle in his blue eyes acknowledging both past efforts and present triumphs. This gathering, once merely a vision, now comes to life before him, vibrant and real. He knows it's just the beginning.

On the other side of the church, Jack Whitmore leads his group with a renewed vigor that mirrors the animated discussions around him. The initially tentative widows and widowers have formed a dynamic circle of friendship and support. Jack's booming laugh punctuates the conversation, and his once somber expression has transformed into one of genuine contentment. "It's never too late for a fresh start!" Jack declares, his words resonant and filled with hope. The group nods in agreement, their enthusiasm a testament to the connection they've forged. Laughter echoes through the room as Jack shares a funny story, his broad shoulders shaking with laughter. The heaviness that once shadowed him has lifted, replaced by a lightness that spreads throughout the group. This ministry, born from shared sorrow, has flourished into a source of joy.

Eleanor Davis stands at the entrance, her posture erect, her tailored clothing crisp and conservative. Her hair is perfectly coiffed, yet her demeanor is soft. She's guiding a group of newcomers, her voice steady and assured as she shares the church's rich history. "These pews," she says proudly, "were hand-carved by our founding families." Her eyes scan the room, filled with nostalgia and fresh excitement.

The sanctuary hums with energy, and Eleanor basks in its transformation. "The updated sound system has made a significant difference," she remarks. She pauses at a newly restored stained-glass window, her gaze lingering as if she were seeing it for the first time.

One of the former members spoke up. Our curiosity is piqued. "And you're really embracing all these changes?" A few nodded in agreement, expressing how the updates have revitalized their sense of community and belonging. Others shared their initial skepticism but admitted that the improvements had brought vibrancy to the sanctuary. Together, they marveled at how these changes had breathed new life into their cherished space.

Eleanor meets their gaze, her expression both thoughtful and determined. "We are," she asserts firmly. "It's not just about where we've been, but about where we're going."

The group's journey winds through the vibrant halls, culminating in the revamped fellowship area. Sunlight streams through the windows, bathing the space in a warm glow. Her voice, once laced with resistance, now carries a hint of anticipation. This church, with its old bones and new skin, is evolving into something beyond what she ever imagined.

As Eleanor rounds a corner, her eyes widen in surprise. Pastor Victor Klaus stands there, a figure from her recent past. His expression is warm, and his presence testifies to the possibility of change. He waves, and his mouth curls into an unassuming smile. "Eleanor," he says, sounding familiar and gentle.

A Community Reborn

Eleanor and Pastor Victor shared a tumultuous history, marked by trauma and division. However, their encounters also shaped Eleanor's journey toward forgiveness and self-discovery. Seeing him now, she is reminded of the lessons learned and the healing slowly beginning to mend her old wounds. She realizes that their past, though painful, had been instrumental in her growth and resilience. The challenges they faced together taught her the importance of empathy and understanding. Standing before him now, she feels grateful for the difficult path that led her to a more compassionate version of herself.

"Pastor Klaus," she replies, her voice softer than she meant. There's a pause, filled with history but not burdened by it.

Since their last meeting, Eleanor has grown considerably, embracing the complexities of her emotions and learning to navigate them gracefully. She has found strength in vulnerability, and her newfound clarity has allowed her to forge deeper connections with those around her. Her journey has not been easy, but it has empowered her to face the future with courage and hope.

"I feel so thankful to be back," he shares, his sincerity shining through every word. She smiles gently, the tension lifting from her shoulders. "We're so happy to have you here! Truly." Her voice conveys a heartfelt apology, though it's unspoken, it resonates clearly between them. Their eyes meet, and a moment blossoms between them. Past grievances begin to fade, like ink dissolving in water. The heaviness of old wounds dissipates, leaving space for something lighter to take root. In this quiet exchange, seeds of forgiveness sprout, their fragile tendrils reaching for the sun. This is a day for grace and renewal—a day for new beginnings.

Oliver stood behind a makeshift podium in an empty lot. A slight man with shaggy gray hair struck a determined pose, holding a battered aluminum guitar. He resembles a wiry statue. A lone black bird swoops low to observe. It is almost certain that this performance is genuine as the young children get closer to it. Their elders keep a respectful distance. Behind him, the rusty hulk of a trailer shudders, then strikes a pose of its own. It held up better than expected. He strummed. The youth inch closer, the mystery of him drawing them in like a haunted house with its lights on. Off to one side, a silver-haired woman carries blueprints like a mother cradling twins. The children, with wide eyes and hesitant steps, are enthralled by the enigmatic figure before them. They whisper among themselves, wondering about the stories hidden within the man's weathered guitar and the tales it might tell.

Each chord he plays seems to weave a spell, pulling them deeper into a world of music and mystery that promises adventure beyond the ordinary.

Jimmy Rodriguez raises his hands, conducting a class as he once did in a bustling schoolroom. However, his orchestra consists of an impromptu gathering of eager young faces. "Keep that rhythm tight!" he calls out, his melodic voice drawing smiles as wide as the sky. A stray dog joins the audience, its head tilted to the side, captivated by the joyful noise. Children sit cross-legged on the sunbaked ground, clapping and singing, their voices growing stronger with every measure. Instruments made from everyday objects—an overturned bucket, a tambourine crafted from bottle caps—fill their laps and the air with possibilities. Jimmy beams at his blended group of intergenerational singers. His heart echoed the hopeful music. "It's not perfect, but it's got soul," he tells a shy boy who looks down at a wrong note. The boy's face brightens, and his fingers are more sure on their next attempt. Laughter and melody fuse into a single entity, sweeping over the lot like a cleansing rain and bringing life to the hard concrete.

Using unconventional instruments adds creativity and innovation to the music, encouraging the children to see potential in everyday objects. It fosters an environment where resources do not limit expression, allowing them to explore sounds in new ways and develop their musical skills. This approach not only enhances their confidence but also nurtures a sense of community and shared discovery as they create something beautiful together.

Fast forward five years. We checked back in with Calvary again during Easter and found Sarah Chen and other leaders as the ministry left the building. The ministry has embraced a more community-focused approach, engaging with local neighborhoods through outreach programs and outdoor gatherings. Sarah and her team have organized various volunteer initiatives, such as food drives and educational workshops, to serve the community's needs better. The shift has allowed the ministry to connect with more people and make a tangible impact beyond the confines of its previous location.

Across town, Sarah Chen manages her crew like an architect directing the construction of a cathedral. Her silver-streaked hair glimmers in the sunlight, and her hands are as active as her mind. She drafts plans and coordinates efforts with the finesse of a maestro. 'We'll have this place looking new in no time," she assures an elderly resident, whose grateful smile reveals a mix of skepticism and hope. The worn shingles and peeling paint that once served as barriers between this woman and her world yield to fresh coats of dignity. Volunteers work in harmony, their chatter resembling the industrious hum of bees, scaffolding dreams with paintbrushes and nail guns. On a weathered porch, Sarah's blueprints are spread out, capturing the curiosity of both the residents and the crew.

"You have quite a vision," comments a young volunteer, his tone filled with admiration.

"It's about respecting the past while making space for the future," she replies, her eyes examining the line between old and new. A soft laugh escapes her as she adds, "Like having one foot in two different worlds and a good sense of balance."

Her touch is precise yet gentle, breathing new life into aged wood and weary spirits alike. The once-dilapidated structures rise with renewed strength, reflecting the transformation of the souls they shelter. Sarah's careful orchestration ensures that nothing is overlooked, from the smallest loose hinge to the largest looming doubt. The project, once an impossible dream, now takes shape, vibrant and real.

In Oakridge, a humble warehouse has become a sanctuary of nourishment. Henry Jenkins stands as a stalwart general amidst the food bank clamor; his organizational skill transforms chaos into order. "Let's keep it moving, folks!" he encourages, his voice booming and efficient at the same time. Volunteers of all ages rally to his call, their hands moving in synchronized generosity. Shelves stocked to overflow create a vibrant palette of hope, each item a brushstroke in the portrait of the community. Families file in, their initial hesitance melting into smiles as they discover more than just food—they find connection and care.

The food bank has become a lifeline for many, providing essential nourishment and stability for those in need. It fosters a spirit of unity and support, bringing together individuals from all walks of life to contribute to a common cause. As a result, the community has grown stronger, with bonds forged through shared experiences and acts of kindness.

"I never thought I'd see this in Oakridge," an elderly man muses to his wife, their arms laden with more than they expected.

Henry oversees everything, with the demands of his hardware store taking a backseat to this new passion. His steady presence inspires confidence not only in those he serves but also in those who work alongside him. The activity swirls like a joyful dance, with every box and bag representing a step toward fulfilling a need, both physical and spiritual. "Remember, we're in this together," he tells a new volunteer struggling with a heavy load. The young man's grin returns, lightening both his burden and his spirit. Henry watches, knowing that this effort, born of faith and determination, nourishes more than just bodies.

Calvary Church's influence spreads through Oakridge like dawn after a long, uncertain night. Outreach programs emerge, not only meeting needs but also transforming the very essence of want. What was once a town gripped by stagnation now breathes with the vibrant air of a second chance. A retired schoolhouse has been repurposed into a community center, its peeling paint a reminder of its past but not its future. Children race through its hallways, their laughter marking territory that was long left unclaimed. A senior center, once quiet and dim, pulses with renewed vigor as its residents gather for weekly game nights and socials. The breadth of Calvary's reach expands far beyond its sanctuary. A thrift store opens, offering clothing and essentials for a pittance and dignity for free. Its racks brim with more than just material; they are infused with the spirit of giving and grace. Another offshoot of the church's vision, a childcare center, hums with youthful energy, its walls adorned with crayon art and filled with hope.

In this mosaic of change, small gestures contribute to the larger picture. Neighbors who once walked past each other in silence now take a moment to exchange greetings and show kindness. A hand-painted sign at the edge of the town of Oakridge is love. The church's commitment to the community is as varied as it is sincere. It touches lives in both expected and unexpected ways. Gratitude becomes a currency that circulates freely, more valuable than any dollar or dime.

In homes, in hearts, and on the streets of Oakridge, Calvary's mission finds fertile ground, planting seeds that blossom into compassion and shared purpose. The landscape, both physical and emotional, shifts from sepia to vibrant hues, with each color serving as a testament to the power of renewal. The final note rings, loud and insistent, reverberating with echoes of itself. As it fades, the surrounding voices diminish too. First come the echoes, then whispers, and finally silence. Outside, children's laughter takes over, followed by the slap of dominoes and the off-key tune of a piano, creating a soundtrack for joyous chaos. Everything transforms into something else as Pastor Terrance and Merle survey the unrelenting bounty that has blossomed. The silence inside becomes laughter, music, and hope. It will be theirs forever if they just believe it.

A Community Reborn

What a transformation five years into the vision being implemented and Calvary's pews empty with the gradual grace of the tide. A mother cradles her newborn, still humming the last of the morning's worship songs. Beside her, an elderly man walks arm-in-arm with a grandchild, their whispers blending in a quiet testament to the day's resonance. The bright-eyed youth from the men's Bible Study rests an arm over a young father's shoulder, their shared jokes and dreams trailing behind them as they leave the sanctuary.

Pastor Terrance McAllister stands by the pulpit, his dark hair catching the morning light, and his eyes filled with a lasting fire. He gazes at the congregation with a smile that resonates deeply within him, welcoming each member like an old friend. Their enthusiasm is contagious, enveloping him and drawing him even closer to this place and its people. "Amen!" shouts a joyful voice, shattering the quiet reverie. Oliver's tousled head pops back through the door, his laughter bouncing off the walls. As families gather and then scatter, Terrance's heart overflows with gratitude. The service has ended, but its spirit lingers, a tangible presence that fills the space with purpose and peace. He steps down from the platform, meeting Beth at the edge of the aisle. Grant, their five-year-old, reaches for him with sticky fingers and a giggle. The church's vitality is their own, and Terrance feels it infusing every fiber of their young family.

As the sanctuary empties, it reveals more than just new colors and repairs. It uncovers a renewal so deep and lasting that it feels like another member of the congregation. The fellowship hall pulses with energy, its vibrant hues and open spaces alive with possibility. A group of young teens gathers in the corner, their heads bent over a shared smartphone. Giggling and exclamations punctuate their reverence with youthful fervor. They text and post pictures, technology and an unexpected accomplice to the community. At a nearby table, a child bangs tunelessly on a piano, her unselfconscious joy an accompaniment to the adults' unhurried conversations.

The expansive lawns outside are bustling with activity, ranging from pickup football games to spontaneous picnics. Blankets dot the grass like islands, each one hosting its own constellation of laughter and camaraderie. An older man pulls out a set of dominoes, the sound of them landing on the picnic table echoing like distant gunfire, sparking laughter. Everywhere, the noise of old things becomes new. It is the sound of Calvary's future, where music, grace, and abundance merge into one unending song.

Amid the buzz, Terrance and Merle Thompson find a moment to step back and take in the view. Merle's weathered face reflects both the history of the church and a spark of enduring hope. He gives Terrance a hearty clap on the back, his wiry frame deceptively strong. "It's something, isn't it?" Merle says, his voice filled with wonder.

"It truly is," Terrance replies, surveying the scene. I knew God had plans for us, but I never imagined this." His gaze sweeps over the crowd, lingering on the once cautious faces that are now open and inviting.

"Everything has come together," Merle reflects, his eyes drifting toward the remodeled wings and revitalized fellowship.

He feels a profound sense of accomplishment and pride in witnessing the transformation that was once just a dream. The revitalized fellowship represents a physical change and a renewed spirit and sense of community. Merle is grateful to everyone who contributed to making this vision a reality.

"Even Eleanor. Inviting Pastor Klaus back." Terrance nods, recalling Eleanor and Klaus's earlier exchange, which fills him with warmth. "Forgiveness can be as transformative as any renovation." They walk the grounds, taking in the joy radiating from each corner.

Forgiveness fosters a sense of unity and understanding, helping to heal old wounds and bring people closer together. It encourages a culture of empathy and support, allowing the community to grow stronger and more resilient. As grudges are let go, individuals feel more connected and motivated to contribute positively to the collective well-being.

Merle gestures toward a group of elderly men discussing an upcoming fishing trip. Their enthusiasm is as unbridled as the younger kids' kickball game."I can't tell who's having more fun," Merle laughed, his voice filled with satisfaction.

Watching the men with their lively banter and camaraderie, Merle felt warmth spreading across his chest. It reminded him of the simple joys of life, moments that transcend age and time. He cherished the sense of community and the shared excitement that lit up their spirits.

"That's the beauty of it," Terrance says, pausing to watch the men. "Everyone's finding their place."

As they make their way to the parking lot, they pass Carolyn and Jonathan Mitchell, their arms loaded with crafts from the children's ministry. "Need a hand?" Terrance offers, but Carolyn waves him off, her smile as warm as the summer air.

"Just keep doing what you're doing, Pastor," she replies, her voice filled with both encouragement and playful teasing. "We can barely keep up."

Jonathan's soft chuckle mirrors hers, his eyes crinkling with appreciation. "It's the good kind of busy."

Merle nods, satisfaction etched in the lines of his face. "A real good kind."

They walk in comfortable silence for a moment, Terrance absorbing the life that spills from every corner. "And Oakridge," he says reflectively, breaking the quiet. "It's changing, too. The church's reach is extending farther than I ever thought possible."

Merle nods, his expression reflecting quiet satisfaction. "It's just like I told you, Terrance. You've planted seeds; you just needed to give them time to grow."

The young pastor's smile widens, and gratitude threads through his every word. "I couldn't have done it without you, without everyone, without God." They stop at the edge of the lot, where they can see the whole scene unfold like a grand, sweeping narrative, its ending as vibrant and hopeful as its beginning. Terrance closes his eyes for a moment, listening to the blend of voices, music, and unrestrained joy that creates the day's refrain. "It required faith," he finally says, opening his eyes and allowing them to rest on Merle. "Faith and patience. But it's happening."

"And this is just the beginning," Merle adds, a quiet certainty in his voice.

Terrance and Merle stand side-by-side, looking over their flock like shepherds. The view is breathtaking and humbling. An expanse of life and hope stretching beyond the horizon. They turn to head back, uplifted by the steadfast promise of what is still to come. In the church's wake, Oakridge blooms like a morning glory, unfurling its petals to embrace the light.

Calvary's revival signifies a rebirth of community spirit and resilience, as it breathes new life into waning traditions and values. It acts as a beacon of hope, drawing individuals from all walks of life to reconnect with their roots and each other. Fostering a shared vision and purpose strengthens the bonds within the community, reminding them of their ability to overcome challenges together.

Discussion Questions

Congregation Gathering:

1. How does the diversity of the attendees at Calvary Church reflect the church's renewed vitality and growth?

Children's Ministry and Community Programs:

2. How does Carolyn Mitchell's dedication to the children's ministry contribute to the church's sense of community and growth?
3. What significance do the various outreach programs, such as Jimmy Rodriguez's music class and Sarah Chen's home repair project, have on the wider Oakridge community?

Personal Transformations:

4. How does Henry's leadership of the men's Bible study and Jack's widows and widowers ministry illustrate the personal transformations within the congregation?
5. What does Eleanor Davis' newfound excitement about the church's renovations and her invitation to Pastor Klaus signify about forgiveness and healing?

Impact on the Community:

6. How has Calvary Church's renewal sparked positive change beyond its walls, and what examples from the chapter highlight this impact?
7. What role does Henry Jenkins' management of the food bank play in embodying the church's commitment to service?

Themes of Renewal and Unity:

8. How do the themes of renewal and unity manifest throughout the chapter, and what moments stand out as particularly significant?

9. What lessons can be drawn from the church's journey in balancing tradition with necessary changes?

Future Prospects:

10. How does the chapter's conclusion with a panoramic view of the church and its surroundings set the stage for the continued journey of Calvary Church?
11. What do you think are the key factors that will determine the success of Calvary Church's ongoing transformation?

www.ingramcontent.com/pod-product-compliance
Lightning Source LLC
Chambersburg PA
CBHW071211160426
43196CB00011B/2263